Skin-Diving Adventures

Skin-Diving

Adventures

By JOHN J. FLOHERTY and MIKE McGRADY

J. B. LIPPINCOTT COMPANY   Philadelphia and New York

Contents

Books by John J. Floherty

FOREST RANGER

TROOPERS ALL: Stories of State Police

MEN AGAINST DISTANCE: The Story of Communications

DEEP DOWN UNDER

SEARCH AND RESCUE AT SEA

GET THAT STORY!: Journalism—Its Lore and Thrills

HIGH, WIDE AND DEEP: Science and Adventure with the Coast and Geodetic Survey

OUR F. B. I.: An Inside Story

TELEVISION STORY

AVIATION FROM THE GROUND UP

WATCH YOUR STEP

FIVE ALARM: The Story of Fire Fighting

SHOOTING THE NEWS: Careers of the Camera Men

BEHIND THE SILVER SHIELD

WHITE TERROR: Adventures with the Ice Patrol

MEN AGAINST CRIME: The Inside Story of T Men

FLOWING GOLD: The Romance of Oil

BEHIND THE MICROPHONE

MONEY-GO-ROUND

By Mike McGrady

CRIME SCIENTISTS

By John J. Floherty and Mike McGrady

SKIN-DIVING ADVENTURES

WHIRLING WINGS

YOUTH AND THE F. B. I.

Skin-Diving Adventures

The New World

FOR MANY YEARS the sea has been our constant companion, our faithful friend. We have lived our lives beside a quiet ocean inlet of even temperament. We have walked beside a happy sea listening to its song of surf against sand. And we have sailed upon an angry sea—a ferocious and bellowing sea lashed by hurricane winds.

Three summers ago we first strapped cylinders of compressed air to our backs. And for the first time we were able to enter *into* the sea.

We found ourselves in a strange new world—the world of the skin diver.

It is a subdued world of peace and tranquillity. The winds may blow and the rains may fall, but the turbulence above is not felt below. The sounds of civilization are muffled and the colors are muted. Even the gravity that anchors man to earth is forgotten.

It is also a jungle—a world of sudden danger and

unexpected violence. The jewel-toned Portuguese man-of-war lives in poisonous harmony with the razor-toothed moray eel. The man-eating sharks swim beside the most vicious animal on earth, the killer whale.

The new world exists beneath ocean and sea, beneath river and lake. Its explorers—over five million of them —are businessmen and scientists, treasure hunters and oil prospectors, housewives and policemen.

We found that skin diving can be as safe as a guided tour through a museum of natural history, as tranquilizing as a leisurely stroll through an exotic garden.

But for many it is as hazardous as the exploration of uncharted wilderness. A Puget Sound skin diver wrestles the many-armed octopus; a Mexican youth stalks three-hundred-pound monster fish with a spear gun; a photographer rubs elbows with a hungry shark, and a treasure hunter uncovers ancient pirate ships; an archaeologist looks for sunken cities, and a scientist searches for knowledge.

This is their story. It is the story of a modern explorer, the adventure-seeking skin diver.

In gathering this material, we traveled from the murky waters of Long Island Sound to the blue seas surrounding Florida's coral reefs, from mountain streams in California to the tideless tranquillity of the French Riviera.

We are indebted to many. We would particularly like to thank the following for their co-operation and support:

Woods Hole Oceanographic Institution;
Scripps Institute of Oceanography;

The Fish and Wildlife Service of the Department of the Interior;

The Department of the Navy;

The Bureau of Ships;

The U.S. Naval School for Underwater Swimmers;

The Office of Naval Research;

The Michigan State Police;

The Underwater Society of America;

The Brooks Institute of Photography;

The Fenjohn Company;

The Boeing Airplane Company;

The Lockheed Aircraft Corporation;

The Bludworth Marine Division of the Kearfott Company, Inc.;

The So-Lo Marx Rubber Company;

The Seamless Rubber Company;

The Garrett Corporation;

The Scott Aviation Corporation;

The Smithsonian Institution;

Eugene D. Vezzani;

Wheeler J. North

W. H. Hamilton, Jr., Commander of the U.S. Navy's Underwater Demolition Unit II.

1. Underwater Hunters

THE DAY OF THE HUNT began peacefully. The Mexican village—a cluster of fishing shacks whitewashed against green slopes—dozed in the mid-morning heat. A fiery sun baked the white beaches of Magdalena Bay, an ocean inlet at the foot of the Lower California peninsula.

There was no hint of trouble on the horizon. There was no warning of the danger waiting in ambush for us.

Paco, our young native guide, met us at the water's edge and outlined his plans for the day's hunt.

"Today we go to the deep water," he said in fluent English. "Today we try for the big fellow."

The "big fellow"—the black sea bass—was a fighting game fish that could weigh as much as three hundred pounds. We planned to stalk this monster—not with rod and reel, but with diving mask and spear gun. Having learned the basic spearfishing techniques on shallow-water fish, we were anxious to begin our first safari for the big game of the underwater world. This was the day we had been waiting for.

We launched Paco's boat into ocean swells blunted by an offshore breeze. The temperamental old outboard motor coughed, hiccuped, chugged into life. Paco steered a northerly course for a deserted section of beach about ten miles from the village of Puerto Cortés.

During out brief trip we saw a fair cross section of the numerous fish inhabiting the clear, warm waters of Magdalena Bay. Albacore and tuna and sheepshead. An ancient turtle glaring at us with sleepy, half-shuttered eyes. Porpoises turning the surface of the bay into a playground, a perfect setting for their aerial gymnastics. There was only one ominous note, the white, sun-bleached bones of a whale decorating the desolate beach.

"The big fellow," Paco said, "he likes to hunt near the rocks. If he sees us coming, he turns and runs away. But don't chase him. Swim along beside him. Then when you are even with him, you turn and shoot."

"Where should we try to hit him?"

"The backbone," Paco said. "Like any other fish. A broadside shot just behind the gills. But don't miss the big fellow. If you hit him in the tail, he will carry you to Japan before he gets tired."

As we continued our trip, we selected our weapons for the hunt. During our earlier practice sessions, we had learned that the spear gun is as deadly a weapon as a high-powered hunting rifle. Paco, our youthful mentor, had stressed safety above all other considerations. He told us that the gun should always be loaded and unloaded in the water. Like a rifle, it must be carried in a point-down position.

We had begun our lessons with the simple hand spear, a long plexiglas shaft with a barbed point—a weapon not unlike that used by the early caveman. This spear, requiring great strength and skill, was soon discarded in favor of the Hawaiian sling—an underwater rifle employing the principle of the bow and arrow. We had then experimented with the spring gun, an Italian import that received its thrust from the release of coiled metal.

This particular day, however, we settled on the arbalete. The most popular of all underwater hunting weapons, the arbalete employs stretched rubber in a manner similar to the slingshot. The four-rubber arbalete, providing tremendous power at close range, is often used for big-game fish.

Spear for underwater hunting is powered by rubber bands. (*Wide World Photos*)

Paco decided to hunt the "big fellow" with his brand-new pneumatic spear gun. Receiving its thrust from the release of compressed air, this submarine "elephant gun" can accurately propel a spear through thirty-five feet of water.

After settling upon the weapons to be used, Paco reached over and cut off the ignition on his outboard motor. We had arrived at our destination. As our sixteen-year-old guide dropped anchor, we noticed that the nature of the shore line had undergone several changes. Large gray boulders had replaced the sand. The water appeared darker and deeper. This was the feeding ground of the "big fellow."

Impatient to begin the hunt, we gathered together the rest of our equipment. After rinsing our swim fins in sea water, we were able to slip them easily over our feet. These webbed rubber foot paddles were designed to give us the greatest possible underwater speed with the least possible effort. Then came the diving masks, our airtight picture windows on the submarine world. We moistened the face plates with saliva, then rinsed them off in order to prevent "fogging."

Finally our most important piece of equipment, the snorkel. This simple plastic breathing tube permits the skin diver to cruise along the surface of the water in a face-down position. We had earlier learned that no self-respecting spearfisherman would ever use an aqualung. SCUBA (Self-Contained Underwater Breathing Apparatus) gives the underwater hunter an unfair advantage over his prey. It would be equivalent to hunting deer with a machine gun from a hovering helicopter.

As we lowered the rope ladder over the stern, Paco offered us a final word of warning.

"When we find the big fellow and hit him, we must take him back to the boat with no delay. Too much blood in the water and *el tigre*—the shark—will come."

With that comforting thought, we climbed down into the warm water of Magdalena Bay. Since the "buddy system" is essential to underwater safety, we began our search in a tight triangular pattern. After accustoming ourselves to breathing through the snorkel tubes, we loaded our spear guns and locked them into the safety position.

Thirty feet of clear water separated us from the sea floor. Our tight-fitting masks permitted us to study a wide variety of fish flitting among the shadowy dark rocks. Groupers mingled freely with small parrotfish. A school of mackerel flashed past the slow-moving snappers. But we saw no fish that resembled the black sea bass.

Maintaining our close search formation, we worked our way in toward the shore. The rocks were patterned by fields of seaweed and intermittent starfish. At a depth of ten feet we turned around and headed for the deeper water. It was then that we received our first scare of the day.

An enormous dark shadow suddenly lifted from the bottom and soared toward us. Terrified, we froze in a stationary position and automatically released the safety catches on our guns.

As the strange animal approached us, we could see that it looked like an oversized bat. Broad and flat, it resembled a refugee from a Hollywood horror movie.

Instead of swimming, it seemed to fly along on wings that stretched twenty feet from one tip to the other.

As we hovered directly above the monster, it suddenly altered course. The wings, rippling smoothly and gracefully, carried the dark shape away from us. It descended again to the bottom and settled like a carpet.

This, Paco later explained, was the manta ray. A distant relative of the shark, the manta is called the "vampire fish" by native fishermen. Although it has an enormous mouth and can weigh over two thousand pounds, the manta will not harm human beings and seldom even hunts large fish.

Thoroughly unsettled, we began our hunt with greater caution. Further search uncovered no traces of the black sea bass, and Paco suggested that we try for some of the groupers before pausing for a rest.

Paco's announcement came as a distinct disappointment. The grouper, one of the easier fish to hunt, is not generally considered a game fish. Clumsy in appearance and slow of movement, the grouper seldom grows larger than fifty pounds. Known as a "homing fish," it tends to feed and live in one spot for days at a time.

Returning to a grouper that we had spotted earlier in the morning, we prepared for the attack. As Paco remained on the surface and watched, we took a deep breath and submerged. Since the grouper tends to flee from a rapidly moving hunter, we approached him with caution.

At first he seemed curious. He hesitated, as if to take a closer look at us. That was the perfect moment to fire. However, our timing was bad. And by the time we had sighted down the barrel of the arbalete and released the trigger on the pistol grip, it was too late.

The spear snaked through the water, trailing its 200-pound test line like a banner, and struck the moving target just above the tail. Having missed any vital organs, the spear seemed to do no damage to the grouper. The fish swam toward a crevice between two rocks and securely wedged himself into the hollow. Although we both pulled on the line, we could not tug the fish from his position.

By this time we were feeling the need for a fresh breath of air and were forced to rise to the surface. After gulping in great breaths, we prepared to descend again for the wounded fish. However, Paco stopped us.

"We must go now," he said.

"Just a minute," we said. "It won't take long to get the fish."

"We must go now," he repeated. "No questions."

Although we did not understand Paco's haste, we nonetheless followed him back to the boat. The thought of leaving a wounded fish and a new spear was repugnant to us—as it would be to any land hunter, who hates waste in any form. As we joined Paco in the boat, he quickly cut off our protests.

"*El tigre*," he said, lapsing momentarily into his native Spanish. "The tiger shark!"

As we followed Paco's gaze, we immediately appreciated the wisdom of his sudden retreat. A single shark, small and similar in appearance to the ground sharks we had often seen in Long Island waters, was slowly circling the wounded grouper. Even as we watched, two other streamlined gray forms joined the first arrival. Then the prominent dorsal fins of a fourth and a fifth

Diver takes a shark for a walk. Tiger sharks fight so fiercely that when captured they go into a state of shock. They will drown unless they are "walked" for several hours, forcing fresh water through the mouth and gills to revive them. Once revived, this shark can be very dangerous. (*Wide World Photos*)

broke through the surface of the water.

"It is better that they eat the grouper," Paco said, with considerable understatement, "than that they eat us."

Since this first encounter we have seen several other sharks at close quarters. While we have never been attacked or even threatened, we have learned to respect this muscular underwater beast. Basically unchanged during the last 350 million years, the shark is a splendidly equipped instrument of destruction. He has an armor of rough, leathery hide, razor-sharp teeth, and an uncanny ability to smell blood at great distances.

Many skin divers laugh at our fears. They assure us that sharks are generally timid and quite unintelligent. Courageous photographers have frightened them away by bumping their cameras against the sharks' ugly snouts. Other skin divers habitually carry wooden staffs to prod sharks that come too close.

In spite of these facts, a skin diver should never relax when a shark is in the vicinity. Two hundred and fifty different varieties of shark inhabit our coastal waters. And while some, like the sixty-foot whale shark, have tiny teeth and will never attack a human, others are confirmed man-killers. Last year there were at least eleven authenticated attacks by sharks off the beaches of the United States.

The danger seems to increase in warm waters, especially when the sky is overcast and the water is murky. Blood from either a wounded fish or an injured human seems to incite this fish to violence. Sharks are especially aggressive during "mob feeding"—when several of them are feasting on the same wounded fish.

While the unarmed skin diver has little defense against an attacking shark, most experts claim that you should never turn your back on him. Some recommend shouting under water. Others claim that the swimmer should attempt to strike the shark's nose with any available heavy object. The chemical shark repellents, such as cupric acetate tablets, offer only temporary protection at best.

There is one safety rule emphasized by all authorities: *don't swim in water containing sharks.*

From our vantage point on the rowboat we could see that the sharks were having greater success in landing the wounded grouper than we had enjoyed. In a matter of moments the battle—and the meal—were over. The thrashing beneath the water stopped suddenly and the sharks slowly drifted away.

Deciding not to risk being added to the menu of any lingering sharks, Paco turned over the motor and guided us to another similar rocky point of land slightly over a mile away. Once again we took up the search for the black sea bass.

While we had no better luck at our new site, we did manage to spot one of his big brothers. The Pacific jewfish, sometimes known as the giant sea bass, has been known to weigh over seven hundred pounds. However, the one we spotted was a mere baby, weighing no more than two hundred pounds.

Paco signaled that he would go after this fish by himself. It would be no easy task. This bloated fish lurked a good forty feet below the surface. Paco would have to dive to that depth, stalk his prey, fire his spear gun, and surface—all on one breath of air.

Treading water on the surface, we studied his every move. What we saw was a living portrait of the expert underwater hunter at work.

After taking a deep breath, Paco ducked beneath the water with hardly a splash. During the first portion of his descent he attained his top speed. As he approached the jewfish, he coasted effortlessly—taking great care to make no sudden movements that would mark him as an aggressor.

As the lean Mexican youth slipped into firing position, the giant sea bass suddenly decided to make a run for his life. The bulky fish burst away from the hunter with a deceptively rapid short sprint.

With any other weapon Paco would not have had a chance. But his pneumatic spear gun saved the day. After quickly sighting down the barrel, Paco squeezed the trigger. This released the compressed air at a pressure of three hundred pounds per square inch. The pressure drove a piston against the spear with sufficient thrust so that the spear was only a blur in the deep water. Fifty feet of white nylon line snaked behind the projectile.

It was a direct hit at a most difficult angle. The spearhead—a triple-pronged point with single-wing barbs—penetrated just inches behind the gills. The fish jerked convulsively and then was still.

Fighting the temptation to surface for air, Paco darted over toward the fish and reached for his spear shaft. Forcing the giant sea bass away from the rocks, he began the tedious process of carrying him up to the surface. As his head broke the water, we swam over to give the young hunter a hand of assistance.

"She's all mine," he gasped, waving us away. "I'll take her in."

Like most other underwater hunters, Paco followed a very strict creed. And one of his prime rules, a rule recently stated by the International Underwater Spearfishing Association, says: "No one may touch any part of the underwater spearfisherman or any part of the equipment already in use at any stage of the catch, or assist in making the catch."

Realizing that he could not hope to boat the fish by himself, Paco decided to drag his catch into shore. As we paddled behind and watched for sharks, the young hunter began the long haul in toward the shore line. The trip to land took the better part of an hour. But the results more than compensated for the efforts. Paco's one fish made a splendid chowder, a fish soup large enough to feed most of our friends in the small village of Puerto Cortés.

Since our first "big-game" hunt we have joined many other spearfishing expeditions. We have seen the hunt for the ferocious moray eel, the tarpon, the barracuda. We have seen the octopus wrestlers of Puget Sound and the aquarium hunters who seek to capture fish without harming them. There are some 30,000 different varieties of fish inhabiting the waters of the world, and many of these fall victim to the underwater hunter.

One of the most remarkable underwater hunting expeditions we ever attended involved no fish at all. And the hunters—two hundred and fifty expert skin divers—carried no spear guns.

The starfish, the colorful, many-armed creature that prowls along the mud of our shallow coastal waters, is actually no relation to the fish. Listed technically as an *Echinodermata*, this innocuous sea animal has no teeth, no visible mouth, and moves with all the speed of a lazy snail. However, it is one of modern man's most bothersome enemies.

This is so because of the starfish's insatiable appetite for oysters. A single starfish, able to attack and devour an oyster twice its size, will demolish several bushels of shellfish during its normal lifetime. It accomplishes this seemingly impossible feat by wrapping its arms around the oyster and exerting a steady pull with hundreds of tiny suckers. As the oyster's shell gradually opens, the starfish then injects some of its tranquilizing digestive juices into the opening. The oyster, temporarily paralyzed, is then quickly consumed.

In past years commercial oystermen made the mistake of chopping the starfish into pieces and then throwing these segments back into the sea. Much to their dismay, they later discovered that each discarded section gave birth to a new starfish.

Consequently the oyster growers of Long Island have turned to local skin-diving clubs for assistance in combating the starfish. On August thirteenth of 1960, over two hundred aqualung enthusiasts invaded the waters of Huntington Harbor with gloves and gunny sacks.

The results of this "Operation Starmop" were amazing.

A petite fourteen-year-old girl named Patricia Cowles managed to carry home 481 of the predatory animals. The real champion of the day, however, was expert diver Bob Maurer, who singlehandedly captured over eight thousand starfish. Before the sun set on this expedition, a half-million starfish were caught and the lives of many millions of oysters were saved.

Another ingenious hunter who does not use a spear gun is a thirty-year-old housewife in the state of Washington. Mrs. Edna Daws, a SCUBA diver for nearly ten years, enjoys nothing better than a meal of succulent lake trout. However, most spearfishermen are banned from our inland lakes and rivers.

Consequently Mrs. Daws had to devise a new method for hunting the trout. We saw this method in operation on the waters of Lake Cushman, a large man-made reservoir at the base of the Olympic Mountains. Instead of using a spear, Mrs. Daws carries a standard trolling line with lead weights, spinners, and baited hook.

After reconnoitering and discovering where the trout are feeding, Mrs. Daws then quite casually drops her regulation fishing line until she has snared enough trout for dinner. She invariably enjoys much greater success than her male counterparts, who do their trolling from boats.

"But doesn't that make the other fishermen angry?" we asked.

"Oh, it did for a while," she said, smiling. "However, I make a practice of surfacing periodically to tell them where the fish are feeding. They're so anxious to get to the new spot that they forget all about being angry."

2. Scuba Troopers

THE GETAWAY CAR—a new white convertible—raced through the winter night. The speedometer needle lay quivering on its right side, but there was no sense of forward motion. The tires seemed to sink into the black-velvet highway, a two-lane ribbon packaging the snow-covered hills of northern Michigan.

"Did you have to shoot him?" the driver asked. "A simple penny-ante job like this. And you, you've got to go and get trigger-happy."

"I *told* you," his companion replied. "I told you he went for his gun first. How was I supposed to know he'd go for his gun?"

"The cops are probably on our tail right now," the driver complained bitterly. "We'll have to ditch the loot. If they catch us with the goods, they'll pin a murder rap on us."

Driving south from the town of Grayling, the driver of the escape car suddenly depressed the brake pedal. The tires squealed as he turned left on a narrow country road and raced toward the shore line of Higgins Lake. Pulling over to the side of the road and cutting the ignition, he stepped quickly from the car. Wasting no time on unnecessary conversation, the two men carried a small bag of coins and bills to the edge of the lake. A thin sliver of January moon reflected softly against the ice that hugged the lake's shore line.

The driver tossed a small weighted bag out past the ice and listened to the splash as it hit the water. He watched with satisfaction as the evidence sank safely out of sight.

"Now your gun," he said, turning to his companion.

"Oh no you don't," the second man protested. "I don't go anywhere without my gun."

"Look, Mac," the leader reasoned, "there's only one place you can go with that gun. And that's straight to the hot seat. If the police find it they'll be able to match it up with the bullet from the body."

"I hate to do it," the second man said. "I'll feel naked without it."

Realizing that the other hoodlum was right, he finally reached into his shoulder holster and removed the murder weapon. Pausing only to kiss it affectionately, he then heaved it well out into the lake.

Their mission accomplished, the two criminals floundered back through the snow to their waiting car. Driving back toward the main highway and freedom, they began to breathe more easily. However, their sense of relief was somewhat premature. They never reached their destination. As they swung onto the main highway, they were met by a cruising patrol car bearing the insignia of the Michigan State Police.

After signaling the two gunmen over to the side of the road, one uniformed trooper left the patrol car and examined the convertible. Holding a light in the driver's eyes, he ordered the two men to leave their car.

"Your car matches the description given by an eye-witness at a shooting in a hunting lodge," the investigating officer said. "I hope you won't mind if I search you."

"Not at all, officer," the driver replied. "Only too happy to help out the law."

The policeman found no weapons on the men and then searched the automobile. Finding nothing, he turned again to the two suspects.

"You boys wouldn't mind telling me what you were doing on that dirt road, would you?"

"Merely sight-seeing, officer," the leader said. "We must have taken a wrong turn."

"Yeah," his companion blurted out his agreement. "You coppers ain't got nothing on us."

"Maybe not yet," the policeman said. "But we'll have to take you in for questioning."

Sullen and silent, the two criminals were taken to a nearby police station and locked up for safekeeping. Then the real work began. Even before dawn the state troopers swarmed into the area and began their search for the missing evidence. They first concentrated their efforts on the undergrowth bordering the highway and then followed the road leading into Higgins Lake.

A mobile crime laboratory arrived at the lake and took plaster castings of the tire tracks and footprints left in the snow. Then a second call went out over the police radio.

This call was relayed to the SCUBA Diving Squad, a recent addition to the Michigan State Police.

The team of skin-diving policemen, assigned to a nearby barracks, arrived at the site of the investigation shortly after the lusterless dawning of a winter day. Each of the Michigan State Police Department's eight regional districts has a team of four or more skilled aqualung divers, and each team has two complete sets of equipment.

Police Sergeants Fred Wilson and Norman Dawson were given this assignment. As they slipped into their cold-water diving suits, the two SCUBA troopers received a briefing from the chief investigating officer.

"We don't know what you'll find out there—if anything," the policeman said. "But we think there may be a revolver and perhaps the money taken from the hunting lodge. Don't take any unnecessary chances beneath the ice. I know you'll do your best; our entire case against those two hoodlums rests on your ability to find the evidence."

Because of the extreme cold, the two troopers wore garments known as wet suits. Constructed of foam neoprene, the flexible suits contained thousands of tiny air pockets. Although a small amount of water could enter beneath the suits, the water was quickly warmed up by body temperature and offered additional insulation against the freezing lake.

Their heads were protected by hoods that permitted the air to enter beneath the garment and flow into the face mask. Their full-shoe swim fins offered additional protection against cold and sharp objects on the bottom of the lake. A combination depth gauge and compass

Two fully equipped skin-diving policemen carefully check each other's diving gear before entering the water in a search for sunken evidence.

was worn on their wrists to avoid confusion while swimming beneath the ice.

The most important piece of equipment for the underwater troopers is, of course, the aqualung. SCUBA (Self-Contained Underwater Breathing Apparatus) consists basically of a tank of compressed air, breathing tubes leading to a mouthpiece, and a system of valves that regulates the flow of air to the diver. Strapped snugly to the diver's back with a harness, it permits the swimmer to move freely through the underwater world with neither the bulk nor the restrictions of the old-fashioned helmet diver.

Sergeants Wilson and Dawson were linked together by a rope, so that there would be no chance of becoming separated in the gloomy water. After chopping an opening in the ice, the two policemen tested their aqualungs and entered the water from the standard horizontal position.

Assuming correctly that the evidence would have been tossed out beyond the ice, they began their search under open water. Almost immediately they saw the handle of the weighted satchel protruding above the silt of the lake bottom. Collecting this valuable piece of evidence, they continued their search for the murder weapon until their supply of compressed air was running low.

Once again on shore, they reported to the officer in charge of the investigation.

"That gun is still out there," Sergeant Wilson said. "Only it must have sunk into the mud."

"Too bad," the ranking officer commented. "That would ensure our case."

"We'll get it," Sergeant Dawson said. "It may take us a little longer, but we'll get it."

After attaching fresh cylinders of compressed air, the two men again entered the icy water. Only this time they carried an additional piece of equipment—a magnetic metals detector. An offspring of the mine detectors developed during World War II, this compact machine weighed less than forty pounds. Using a three-foot probe, it was able to locate objects made of ferrous metal at a considerable distance.

Once again they took up the search. Before five minutes had passed, the magnetic metals detector signaled the presence of an object beneath the mud. As Sergeant Wilson held the machine, Sergeant Dawson reached into the silt with his gloved hands. Frantically scooping with both hands, he dug up the metal object and lifted it above the clouded water.

It was a rusted tin can discarded by picnickers the previous summer.

Undaunted, the SCUBA troopers returned to their task. Approximately thirty feet past the site of the discarded money they received a second reaction. This time there was no necessity to dig deep into the soil. Just a few inches beneath the surface they found a snub-nosed .45-caliber revolver that had not yet had a chance to accumulate a coat of rust.

The search was over. Ballistics experts in the East Lansing police laboratory later proved that the weapon was the same one used for the murder. Faced with this evidence, the two men pleaded guilty to the crimes of murder and armed robbery.

This story—currently being repeated in many of our most modern police departments—attests to the skill and efficiency of the underwater patrolman. Michigan, with its 11,000 lakes and 40,000 square miles of water, has made an ideal proving ground for the SCUBA trooper.

The Michigan program began back in 1957 with a class of sixteen hand-picked troopers. During an intensive five-day, dawn-to-dusk training period, these men learned how to combine their skin-diving hobby with their chosen profession of law enforcement. The following year nineteen new divers were trained. And today the squad boasts a strength of sixty men.

During a recent visit to East Lansing, we had an opportunity to observe a new class of officers being trained in the use of the aqualung. The first words we heard—spoken by Lieutenant William Ward of the Police Training Bureau—emphasized the serious nature of this particular brand of skin diving.

"You are Michigan State troopers who are water specialists," Lieutenant Ward said. "You are not skin divers who just happen to be state troopers."

The men chosen for the squad are never permitted to forget that diving is a serious and sometimes deadly part of their business. Corporal Bill Carter, the head of the entire diving operation, emphasized this fact in a conversation.

"We take only men who are in top shape," Corporal Carter told us. "And they must stay that way. Even

Candidates for the Michigan State Police SCUBA diving squad receive instructions in the use of diving equipment.

after completing their training, the men are expected to spend a great deal of their free time practicing in nearby lakes and rivers."

A second, equally important, requirement is a sense of dedication.

"We offer no promise of extra pay or promotion," Corporal Carter told us. "We offer no release from regular duties. We offer only hard work and a chance to serve the public."

The training program for the newly chosen SCUBA troopers begins in the safety of the police department's regular swimming pool. The students first learn the correct and safe way to master the aqualung. They then proceed to the basic activities involved in diving, first aid, technique of pattern searching, underwater geology, and survival swimming.

"The emphasis is always on safety," Corporal Carter said. "These men must be able to handle any emergency. They learn 'buddy-breathing'—two divers sharing the same breathing supply. They are restricted to a depth of sixty-six feet to avoid unnecessary risk. And special departmental permission is required to exceed that depth."

Today the SCUBA troopers are firmly established as a vital arm of the Michigan State Police. Last year the divers went out on seventy underwater investigations. During the course of their work they recovered twenty-seven drowned persons and thirty-two articles of criminal evidence.

Their underwater searches cover a wide range of objects. One excursion was a hunt for a two-million-dollar Air Force jet that sank in Saginaw Bay. Another assignment, involving no crime, resulted in the recovery of two pairs of eyeglasses inadvertently lost by ice fishermen.

Michigan's pioneering performance is being repeated in every corner of the nation. During a recent visit to New Jersey, we picked up an emergency call on the police radio. The call was directed to the Underwater Recovery Service of the New Jersey State Police.

"Man believed drowned. Man believed drowned," the radio voice repeated tonelessly. "Rush all equipment to Beach Haven. Repeat. Rush all equipment to Beach Haven."

Since we were near the indicated area, we drove quickly to Long Beach, a thin strip of land separating the calm waters of Barnegat Bay from the Atlantic Ocean. Motoring into the small resort village of Beach Haven, we discovered that a police emergency van had beaten us to the scene.

The officer in charge outlined the situation.

"It looks as if a fisherman may have drowned while he was surf-casting in this area," he said. "Witnesses say he was standing here all day. He disappeared about an hour ago. We found his hat, one boot, and his casting equipment. They were washed ashore by the breakers. Now it's up to our skin divers. They'll have to go in and see if they can find the body."

The SCUBA troopers, arriving several moments later, found all the necessary search equipment in the emergency van. In addition to the diving suits and aqualungs, there was also an air compressor for refilling the air cylinders and a supply of portable, battery-powered underwater floodlights.

Six skin-diving patrolmen donned the equipment quickly and silently. Their grim faces reflected the solemnity of the assignment. The entire procedure had obviously been well rehearsed, and the men exchanged few words as they formed a close-interval search pattern and walked into the ocean.

Skillfully avoiding the impact of the breakers, the men entered the water and reformed the grid pattern that they would maintain throughout the search for the drowned man.

Crowds from nearby resorts arrived at the scene, and the police were forced to construct rope barriers. As twilight became night, we could clearly see the underwater floodlights operated by the SCUBA troopers. The searching party returned empty-handed after approximately a half hour of work to replace their cylinders of air.

One observer, a small, balding gentleman with a gaily colored sport shirt, stood beside us, puffing on an old-fashioned bowl pipe. He seemed quite interested in the entire procedure. Another spectator turned toward us, examined our small neighbor, and paled as though he had seen a ghost.

"That's the man!" he shouted to the police officer. "That's the man who was fishing here! That's the man who drowned!"

The officer in charge of the search party stopped the underwater policemen just as they were entering the water a second time. He then walked over toward us. In his hand he carried the surf-casting rod and the boot washed ashore by the waves.

"Do these belong to you?" he asked the small man.

"They did belong to me," the man said.

"They *did?* What do you mean by that?"

"Well, it's a long story," he answered, puffing thoughtfully on his pipe. "You see, I've been fishing here all day—ever since sunrise—and not one bite. So I finally got disgusted."

"You mean you threw your equipment away?"

"That's right," he agreed. "I had no idea you were looking for me. I hope this didn't cause you any trouble."

"Any trouble," the police officer repeated—then finally smiled. "No, not really. I only wish that all our underwater searches had a happy ending. Unfortunately, they don't."

3. Underwater Prospector

THE BUS COMPLAINED in the chill of dawn like an arthritic old lady. It had carried us from the elbow-rubbing buildings of San Francisco, past the lush green fields surrounding Sacramento, and was now climbing slowly into the mountains of Tahoe National Forest.

In all probability we were off on a wild-goose chase. A telegram—terse, mystifying, irresistible—had been delivered to our hotel room a day earlier.

> FINALLY STRUCK IT RICH. TAKE MORNING
> BUS TO CISCO SPRINGS. BRING DIVING SUITS.
> WILL EXPLAIN THEN. WHOOPEE!
>   WILL BURTON

Will Burton was no stranger to us. We had met him many times during our reporting for past books. A professional adventurer, this thirty-one-year-old ex-Marine is an enthusiastic skin diver and an incurable treasure hunter. During the past decade he had prospected for oil off the Gulf of Mexico, searched for sunken Spanish galleons in the Bahamas, joined a salvage party at the site of the sunken luxury liner *Andrea Doria*.

However, this was the first time that Will Burton had ever mentioned striking it rich. We had no idea what he was doing in Sierra County, California. We realized, of course, that this was the site of the first great gold rush over a century ago. But it was difficult to imagine Will Burton bending over a mountain stream with a gold miner's pan in his hands.

Our bus groaned to a stop before the town depot. We were the only two passengers to step down. We stretched and looked around. Cisco Springs, a mere dot on the California road map, was not much larger in real life. We had no difficulty locating Will Burton. His broad-shouldered frame represented the only sign of life on the town's main thoroughfare.

He began to speak even before reaching us.

"Gold," he said. "Gold. All you want. Just lying there for the taking."

"Aren't you about a hundred years too late?"

"Too late? You come along with me and you'll see who's too late."

Will had been in Cisco Springs just long enough to purchase a "grubstake"—flour, lard, coffee, dried eggs, dehydrated potatoes, and tins of meat and vegetables. These supplies were loaded into the back of a pickup truck for the first leg of our journey. And after a drive over paved and dirt roads, these supplies were then strapped onto the backs of two burros—sullen, stubborn animals who obviously failed to share Will's enthusiasm for the trip.

Our trek—by auto and by foot—carried us into the

heart of the "mother lode," a narrow strip of gold-rich land reaching 120 miles into the foothills of the Sierras. There was an air of unreality about the entire area. It had undergone many changes since 1848, when a man named James Wilson Marshall found those first flakes of gold in the American River.

This set off one of the greatest gold rushes in history. Many thousands of treasure seekers poured into the "mother-lode" country. The first bearded prospectors panned gold by hand, then constructed makeshift sluices.

Then came the enormous mining corporations with their heavy machinery. They sank shafts deep into the bowels of the earth. They dammed up rivers, changed their courses, scraped the gold from the dry river beds. They brought in hydraulic washes and flushed away hillsides. And through the years they carved two billion dollars' worth of gold from the soil.

But when the gold ran out the boom towns died a quick death. We encountered only ghost towns, pathetic shadows of the flourishing cities of a century ago. The streets are never straight; hastily built, they invariably follow the twisting course of a nearby stream. The buildings are decayed, the stone walls are broken, and the locust trees are choked by a thick tangle of undergrowth.

Our trail took us past these deserted towns, past the simple stone monument at Sutter's Sawmill, where it all started, past the roads and into the forest. When we stopped for our afternoon meal, the sun had already begun its downward course toward the horizon.

"Sure is beautiful country," Will remarked.

"Sure is," we agreed. "But we never knew you were

such an admirer of mountain scenery. We never thought we'd live to see the day when you'd give up skin diving."

"Who's giving up skin diving?" Will scoffed. "I asked you to bring your diving suits, didn't I?"

"So you did," we recalled. "Your telegram also said that you had struck it rich. Not that we doubt your word, Will, but how would a skin diver strike it rich in the mountains?"

"You'll see soon enough," he promised. "And if you don't believe me, this may convince you. It'll show you how much I've made during the past eleven weeks."

He handed us a bankbook. We flipped it open and examined the first page. The printed figures indicated that one Mr. William Burton had made three deposits during the past four months. The total of these deposits showed that he had managed to accumulate a magnificent total of sixty-seven thousand dollars.

This effectively muffled all further skepticism on our part. Now impatient to proceed with our excursion, we rose to our feet and began to prod the burros. However, since we were at an elevation of over a mile, we were forced to stop and rest the animals periodically. Not until sunset did we arrive at the end of the route.

Below us, carving a silver trail through the forestland, was the north branch of the American River. The sun, hastening toward its fiery rendezvous with the West, cast golden shadows on the woodland—the firs and oaks, the yellow pines and yellow-berried madroña trees.

We followed Will down the incline to the river and prepared camp for the night. The rush of white water racing over smooth rocks, the cheerful snap of the campfire hushed the mournful plea of a lonely owl. We sat back and enjoyed the peace of dusk descending on the mountains.

"It won't be this quiet for long," Will predicted. "When the others find out, there'll be a rush up here like you can't imagine. It'll make '49 seem like small potatoes."

"Find out about what?"

"About the gold, of course," he replied. "After all, I'm not the only one who's been prospecting. I've heard of some big strikes down on the Yuba River. On the Feather River too."

"Big strikes? We thought the forty-niners had taken all the gold out of these streams."

"That's what everyone else thought," Will chuckled. "But they were all mistaken. The forty-niners did take a lot of gold out of here. But they couldn't get it all. They left plenty, plenty to go around."

"Fine—but how do you get it?"

"Tomorrow," he said, tapping the ashes from his pipe. "Tomorrow morning you'll find the answers for all your questions."

The night became bitterly cold, and we placed fresh logs on the fire. As we settled down in our sleeping bags, we studied the warm flickerings of the blaze against the overhead branches. Sleep was slow in coming that night. Thoughts of gold glinted through our dreams. And the next thing we knew, Will was shaking us into wakefulness.

"Time to get up," he announced. "Can't have you sleeping all day long."

After managing to pry open our eyes, we consulted our watches. It was not quite six o'clock. However, the smell of frying bacon and boiling coffee caused us to rise without protest. After breakfast we followed Will several hundred yards downstream.

We immediately saw all the traditional prospecting apparatus—basins, picks, a sluice, crowbars, and shovels. In addition there were several larger pieces of machinery. The final piece of equipment was the skin diver's cold-weather diving suit.

"That's right," Will finally explained. "Skin diving—that's how we get the gold. We just dive into the river and pick up the nuggets that the old prospectors couldn't reach."

Noticing the absence of any aqualungs, we asked Will how he managed to breathe while searching for the gold.

"Aqualungs would only get in the way," he said. "We'd have to keep refilling them. That's why I've got all this machinery here. It's used for Hookah—it pumps air down from a compressor directly to the diver's mouthpiece. The same motor that operates the air compressor also provides power for a portable dredge."

"Why do you bother with the diving suits?"

"Wouldn't last long without them," he said. "This water comes from melting snow up on those mountains."

As we tugged our rubber diving suits over our winter-weight underwear, Will explained why he had settled upon this particular spot.

"This should be good pickings," he said. "This was once mined with big hydraulic washes that gouged the soil from both sides of this valley. They could get only about fifty per cent of the gold that way. And, by my calculations, that leaves approximately fifty per cent for us."

During our first trip into the deep pool of icy green water we carried no tools. Before joining Will in the actual prospecting, we wanted to acclimate ourselves to this strange new underwater endeavor. We discovered that the Hookah breathing process was no more difficult than SCUBA. However, there were certain limitations. We could go no farther than the length of our flexible breathing tube would permit.

We soon learned that there was no need to go any farther. Will Burton bent down and dislodged a large stone from its resting place. Reaching his hand into the gravel, he extracted a nugget of gold as large as a marble.

Convinced now that this was, indeed, "good pickings," we followed Will to the surface and waited impatiently for our assignments.

"There's gold in them thar hills," he said, smiling. "Now I'm going to show you how we get it. You'll have to learn how to use this—it's the most important piece of equipment we have."

As he spoke, he pointed to a small piece of machinery that was connected to the motor generating power for the air compressor. The apparatus was linked to a long arm of hose that ended in an aluminum nozzle.

"This is our portable dredge," he explained. "It's just like a vacuum cleaner. Only instead of taking dust from a carpet, it picks up gold from a river bottom. You'll have to come along and watch at first. Then, once you get the hang of it, you can try it yourselves."

Our next trip down was strictly for observation. We

noticed that Will held the aluminum grip of the nozzle in his left hand. The mouth of the nozzle, two inches in diameter, was directed into crevices and irregularities on the river bottom—underwater vaults that might safely have stored nuggets for centuries. The gravel that lined these apertures was rapidly sucked into the hose and washed up onto the surface.

There the mixture of water and rocks was jetted out onto a separating board and then funneled into the sluice. As Will continued "vacuuming" the river bed, we went ashore and watched the filtering process. The final stage involved the use of a riffle box, the container designed to capture the heaviest particles. Since gold is one of the heaviest metals, it sank into the mesh while the pebbles were washed away.

During the next hour we remained above the water and collected the gold, while Will did the heavy work down below. In our eagerness we managed to amass a small fortune in glittering rocks before he came up to inspect our progress.

"Quite a haul," he commented.

We could only agree with him.

"There's just one trouble," he said. "Most of that is plain old fool's gold."

Chagrined, we stepped back and watched his skillful fingers probe our collection and extract a half-dozen genuine nuggets. He placed these in a wide-mouthed glass jar and casually tossed the rest of our "small fortune" into the rapids.

"About two ounces of gold," he estimated.

"Two ounces? Is that all?"

"Oh, that's not so bad," he replied. "About sixty

dollars' worth. Where else can you earn sixty dollars an hour?"

We had no ready answer to that. However, we soon learned that even at sixty dollars an hour, this form of gold mining could be a discouraging operation. After Will's initial dredging, the backbreaking phase of the operation began. We pried aside all the larger rocks with crowbars and then turned over the bottom land with pick and shovel. This kind of physical labor is tough enough when done on dry land. When the worker must also combat swift currents, near-freezing temperatures, and impenetrable bedrock, he knows he'll never again complain about weeding a garden.

The rewards for our labors during the first two days more than compensated for the blistered hands and aching backs. However, on the third day the gold suddenly vanished. Entire hours passed by without a single strike. Covering nearly a half mile of river, we didn't find enough gold to pay for the gasoline that powered our air compressor.

Shortly before sunset we discovered the reason. We had been mining a portion of the river that the forty-miners had once dammed up. The water had been temporarily diverted from its normal route, and the early prospectors had thoroughly cleaned the gold from the dry river bed.

And before our week of underwater prospecting ended, we were to encounter all the standard skin-diving hazards—as well as a few treacherous refinements. Sierra County, long noted for its forest fires, treated us to one of its minor productions. Forced to stop work for a full day, we battled the blaze beside crew members airlifted to the territory via a Forest Service helicopter.

However, most of the danger was found beneath the water. On the day of our departure Will led us to a deep pool at the base of a miniature waterfall. The falling water churned one end of the pool white and created a strong whirlpool at the point of impact. Pointing this out, Will advised us to remain a safe distance from the deep side.

Only too happy to oblige, we concentrated our efforts in the relative safety of the shallows. However, even at that distance we could feel the pull of the waterfall and the second tug of the current racing from our end of the natural reservoir.

Suddenly we noticed that Will Burton was no longer with us. His breathing tube, apparently jerked from his mouth, sank to the bottom. We realized that there was no time for delay—remaining in close contact, we waded into the deep end of the pool. The suction force of the water became increasingly strong. Luckily our air hoses effectively tethered us, preventing us from coming too near that subsurface tornado of white bubbles. However, we were close enough to peer through the curtain of twisting foam and see that Will Burton was not there.

That left but one alternative. He must have been washed away by the downstream current. Edging cautiously away from the waterfall, we retraced our steps. Discarding our face masks, we followed the pebbled riverbank past several hundred feet of twisting rapids.

We finally found Will Burton. He was sitting calmly

against a half-submerged log in a calm eddy on the side of the river. Reaching up to an overhanging bush, he was casually plucking berries and popping them into his mouth.

"Are you all right?" we asked. "Are you hurt?"

"Hurt?" He seemed surprised by our question. "Not at all. I just thought I'd take me a little swim. Of course, it did get a mite rough back there."

We looked back at the trail he must have followed to reach his present position. It was a pounding roller-coaster ride between ominous black rocks. Closer examination revealed several long gashes through his rubber suit. However, almost miraculously, that was the extent of the damage. Will Burton rose to his feet unassisted and, limping only slightly, returned to his work as though nothing had happened.

Limping ourselves—from fatigue, not injury—we happily returned to civilization the following morning. During our week with Will we had managed to bring in almost a thousand dollars' worth of dust and nuggets. Although this seemed like quite adequate pay for a week of excitement and adventure, Will Burton didn't share our elation.

"Worst week so far," he muttered. "If you stay up here a while longer you might be able to pick up some real pocket money."

However, Will's underwater prospecting in the mother-lode country had almost come to an end. He and the other early arrivals could not expect to keep their secret forever. Since nothing causes more excitement than the news of a gold strike, the pioneering gold seekers found themselves joined by hundreds of other skin divers.

And now most of the California rivers have been mined out a second time. Dealers who specialize in the sale of portable dredges and air compressors report that they are running a full year behind their orders. Even the cost of the equipment—generally in the neighborhood of six hundred dollars—does not seem to discourage the underwater prospectors.

Although most of the larger strikes were made by the first submarine miners, an occasional find will still cause a flurry of renewed interest and activity. One skin diver recently hauled out one-hundred-thousand dollars' worth of gold during his summer vacation. And two enterprising teen-age boys, skin diving under a bridge over the Yuba River, managed to extract three thousand dollars' worth of nuggets during just one particularly memorable afternoon.

However, as the competition increases, these success stories become fewer and fewer. Since the modern sourdough cannot legally file a claim on a river, news of a strike will attract hundreds of eager skin divers in a matter of days.

Other SCUBA prospectors, dismayed by the overcrowded condition, are now turning their eyes toward the sea.

Rain has been falling, on and off, for many millions of years. This eternal rainfall has washed countless tons of minerals into the rivers, and the rivers have carried them to the oceans. Underwater volcanoes have belched mineral-rich discharges into the sea since the beginning of time. As a result, today's oceans are vast strongboxes storing much of the world's natural wealth.

Man, however, has been unable to find the key that will unlock this strongbox.

Gold, the glittering lure that attracts all prospectors, is locked there in unimaginable abundance. Each cubic mile of ocean contains nearly one hundred million dollars' worth of fine gold particles—enough to make every man, woman, and child a millionaire.

Today, however, the underwater prospector can only dream of the day when science develops a practical method for recovering this gold. Not that all the ocean's wealth is out of his reach. Quite the contrary. Some of the most exciting finds of the past decade have been made by underwater prospectors searching for oil off California and the Gulf of Mexico. This story, the story of the search for "black gold," is related in this book's final chapter.

Will Burton, a man who has successfully prospected for both oil and nuggets, has no plans for retirement. The last time we saw him he was occupying a suite of rooms in San Francisco's finest hotel. During a two-week vacation he was dining in the best restaurants, seeing the newest plays, and making plans for the future.

"What will you do now?" we asked. "Now that you're a wealthy young man?"

"You won't tell anyone?" he asked.

"Just our readers," we replied.

"Well, all right," he said, smiling. "I was thinking of taking a little trip. Thought I might visit one of our newest states."

"Hawaii?" we guessed.

"Alaska," he said. "Those early prospectors on the Yukon probably weren't any smarter than the forty-niners. I think I'll just mosey on up to Skagway and see if they forgot anything on the bottom of the river."

4. The Frogmen

THE TRANSOCEANIC LINER cruised from the restless gray waters of the Atlantic into the mouth of the Mediterranean Sea. We had been through a rough crossing, and the great ship stopped at Gibraltar for a two-day layover. After gathering together our skin-diving equipment, we debarked and motored up the Spanish coast toward Málaga.

Everywhere we encountered the sunlit serenity of a sparkling spring morning. Black-shawled, busy-fingered women sat on the sandy beaches and repaired fishing nets. Their leather-faced husbands loaded freshly caught sardines into cannery carts. And across the water we could see the shadowy purple outline of North Africa.

We stopped at the small fishing village of Fuengirola for lunch. Unable to resist the lure of the sea any longer, we followed the cobbled road down to the shore. After donning our masks and fins and snorkels, we waded out into the water.

The Mediterranean lived up to all advance notices.

The water, astonishingly blue from a distance, was clear and warm. Free of tide and current, it pressed gently against the white sands and black rocks. This was, indeed, a skin diver's paradise.

Yet just two decades ago this same water was justifiably known as a diver's hell.

For it was in these now-peaceful waters that modern underwater warfare first became a grim reality. In this very spot skin divers once met in deadly hand-to-hand combat. And it was here that the twentieth-century frogman received his baptism by fire.

The year was 1942. World War II had begun. The Allies were gradually pushing the enemy forces from the African deserts. Suddenly and unaccountably, British ships carrying troops and supplies through the narrow Gibraltar gateway were being attacked and destroyed.

The ships literally never knew what hit them. There were no enemy vessels in the vicinity. The recently developed sonar radarscopes showed no trace of lurking submarines. Yet 150,000 tons of battleships and merchant vessels sank to watery graves.

The answer to this lethal riddle was finally found beneath the surface of the water. Enemy frogmen— riding giant torpedoes like cowboys on ponies—were singlehandedly severing the vital lifeline linking the supply depots with the Allied desert forces. Sitting astride fifteen-foot "tin fish," the human torpedoes were able to accomplish more damage than the entire enemy navy.

The courageous enemy frogmen, led by a bold lieutenant, used the Spanish seaport of Algeciras as their

base of operations. Guiding their explosive vehicles to
the hulls of British ships, the small band of torpedo
pilots waited until the last possible moment before
swimming frantically away from the ensuing explosions.
Although there seemed to be madness in their methods,
there was also method in their madness. The Allied
forces seemed powerless against the dedicated and sui-
cidal unseen enemy.

The British Navy, determined to halt the series of
mysterious underwater explosions, promptly dispatched
a one-man investigating committee to Gibraltar.

This crucial assignment was given to a most unlikely
candidate—a youthful lieutenant with dark, wavy hair,
sharp, well-defined features, and absolutely no enthusiasm for water sports. By his own admission, the new
Mine and Bomb Disposal officer had difficulty navigat-
ing the length of a swimming pool under his own power.

Italian frogmen attaching warhead by clamps to bilge keels
during World War II.

That man was Lieutenant Lionel Philip Kenneth Crabb, one of Britain's greatest naval heroes.

Despite his aversion to swimming, Lieutenant Crabb immediately realized that he would have to meet the enemy on his own grounds. And those grounds were beneath the night-darkened waters of the Mediterranean.

This proved to be no easy task. The new officer and his small squad of fledgling frogmen had no modern diving apparatus. Only heavy-weight winter underwear protected them against the cold. Their feet were covered by lead-soled tennis shoes. The only underwater breathing apparatus then available was the Davis Submerged Escape Apparatus, an oxygen container designed solely for use by men escaping from sunken submarines.

Despite this the small band of underwater demolitionists entered the water every night in search of mines deposited by the well-equipped enemy. Working with knives and nerves, they managed to deactivate hundreds of submarine bombs left by their foe.

Shortly after his arrival the new lieutenant received one of his toughest assignments. A British airplane, a Liberator flying from the Middle East to England, crashed and sank in Gibraltar Harbor. Among its seventeen passengers, the ill-fated aircraft had carried the famed Polish war hero, General Sikorsky.

When news of the crash reached British authorities, an urgent message was relayed to Lieutenant Crabb. The dispatch revealed that General Sikorsky had been carrying a briefcase filled with secret documents. Should the enemy forces obtain these papers, "it would prove detrimental to the entire war effort."

Frogmen of the British Royal Marines go to school. *(British Information Service)*

This same information was simultaneously cabled from Axis headquarters to their wartime partners. Thus began one of the strangest underwater races in history. As Lieutenant Crabb's underwater warriors plunged into the water from Gibraltar, their enemy counterparts began a similar expedition from the Spanish shore line.

The two groups met at the site of the downed airplane.

Crabb and his men, armed with knives and wrecking tools, turned to meet the adversary in hand-to-hand combat. Hastily deciding that discretion was, indeed, the better part of valor, the enemy squad backed down and retreated from the area.

However, their retreat was only temporary. As the English frogmen began the gruesome and time-consuming task of removing the drowned passengers of the aircraft, the foe plotted a counterattack. They realized that the British would be forced to spend several days combing the wreckage for every scrap of paper, every particle of microfilm. So, returning to the sunken plane at night, the enemy frogmen fastened two underwater time bombs to the wreckage and then departed.

Fortunately Lieutenant Crabb discovered the mines before they were due to explode. The new "limpet mines," clamped to the plane's metal skin like limpet clams adhering to a rock, were unlike any that Lieutenant Crabb had ever seen.

Removal would be, at best, a risky task. There was no way of knowing whether they were equipped with booby traps, devices that would cause them to detonate while being removed. However, there was only one way to find out—that was to remove them.

After waving his squad to safety, Lieutenant Crabb swam up beside the mines and examined them at close range. He discovered that they were attached to the metal by three clamps that could be loosened only with considerable effort. Proceeding slowly and cautiously, the heroic frogman began to loosen the clamps. Although each counterclockwise twist of the screws might mark the end of his life, the lieutenant did not hesitate.

Before he could finish his deadly job, his supply of oxygen gave out, and he was forced to surface for a fresh supply and an uncontaminated canister of the soda lime used in filtering out the poisonous carbon dioxide. Exhausted and trembling beneath the strain, Lieutenant Crabb returned to complete the process of removal. To his relief, he discovered that the mines carried no booby traps.

However, removal was only the beginning of his work. As his men watched in amazement, he then towed the time bombs out into the open sea and proceeded to attack them again—this time with screw driver and wrench. Realizing that he would encounter many more of these mines in the future, the courageous lieutenant had decided to disarm the novel mines and examine their inner workings.

Although only minutes passed before he managed to dismantle the detonating mechanisms, Lieutenant Crabb was to recall later that this first flirtation with death seemed to endure "slightly longer than an eternity."

During the course of World War II, the Lieutenant was to suffer through many such eternities. The raw young lieutenant with little swimming ability later emerged as a full commander and one of the most decorated heroes in British history. His repeated acts of bravery ultimately merited him the coveted King George Medal.

The career of the world's most famous frogman ended tragically beneath a cloak of mystery in April of 1956. During that month the political rulers of the Soviet Union sailed into Portsmouth Harbor aboard the cruiser *Ordzhonikidze*. And during that same month a man with dark, wavy hair and well-defined features checked into Portsmouth's Sallyport Hotel under an assumed name.

That man was Commander Lionel Crabb. And this was to be Crabb's last dive. Newspaper reports have claimed that he was there on a secret government mission, an espionage assignment with the aim of spying on the Russian cruiser from an underwater vantage point. Commander Crabb never emerged from the water. Most observers feel that he was detected and killed during the performance of his duty. Other reports—based on hazy photographs and intercepted Soviet messages—claim that he was captured and is now held prisoner within the Soviet Union.

Only one thing is certain. Commander Crabb will be missed. British government official Hugh Gaitskell summed up the sentiments of the entire free world during a eulogy delivered to the English Parliament: "Whatever may be the circumstances in which he met

Underwater demolition crew coming ashore after period of strenuous diving. (*U.S. Navy Photo*)

his death, all of us will agree that this country would be the poorer were it not for men like Commander Crabb."

Although Crabb is the most famous modern frogman, underwater warriors have been used since five hundred years before the birth of Christ. Xerxes, a monarch of ancient Persia, used divers to wreck enemy ships. And during the siege of Syracuse, Athenian swimmers were used to chop down harbor barriers. Alexander the Great, one of the most famous of the early diving enthusiasts, used a team of skin divers to shatter the defenses constructed beneath the harbor of Tyre.

The first American underwater warriors were deployed against British warships during the Revolutionary War.

However, the modern frogman was not added to this country's arsenal until well after Commander Crabb's pioneering work at Gibraltar. Our first UDTs—Underwater Demolition Teams—were selected from the Seabees during May of 1943.

These frogmen were later used during every major invasion of the latter phases of World War II. On the beaches of Tarawa and Guam and Normandy the UDTs distinguished themselves in what may have been the most hazardous of all wartime assignments. In addition to the ever-present threat of enemy bullets, they regularly faced the added dangers of subfreezing polar waters and shark-infested tropical seas. During the first hour of the Omaha Beach invasion in Normandy, the frogmen lost fifty per cent of their personnel.

Despite the danger to their lives, the UDTs did their job and did it well. Their role during the invasion of

Guam typifies the courage, efficiency, and enthusiasm that accompanied their every assignment.

Guam, the largest of the Mariana Islands, had been seized by the Japanese during the opening days of the war. Strategically situated south of Japan and east of the Philippines, this enemy stronghold was one of our nation's prime military objectives during the summer of 1944.

The first men to arrive at Guam were, naturally enough, the frogmen. Three weeks before the actual attack an Underwater Demolition Team thoroughly reconnoitered the beaches of Guam. Armed only with compasses, depth gauges, and plastic mapping apparatus, the men charted the locations of mine fields and shore defenses. Upon returning to headquarters, they decided that the coral-encrusted Assan Beach would be the most vulnerable site for attack.

Then, operating under cover of night, the UDTs returned to Guam a second time. This trip was for the purpose of removing and deactivating all enemy mines planted in the area.

The preliminaries out of the way, the frogmen made many other trips to the site of the planned invasion. A speedy Navy PT boat deposited them well off shore and the underwater warriors swam toward the beach with a deadly cargo. Trailing behind the expert swimmers were submerged canvas bags filled with TNT. Before this one mission ended, they had carried in over five tons of explosives.

The dynamite was attached to obstacles erected by the enemy and then to the six hundred coral cribs that might obstruct the invading force. A time-delay fuse

Among the hazards of the skin diver's profession is the placing of large quantities of explosives. *Above, left*, a member of an Underwater Demolition Team, wearing a sand-colored suit, attaches a package of TNT to the base of a bridge. Time-delay fuse links explosive with underwater detonator. *Above, right*, shows the demolition blast of a sunken wreck. *(U.S. Navy Photos)*

Below, braving icy Arctic waters and falling snow, divers from U.S.S. DELIVER repair injured propellor at Sheppards Bay, Canada. *(U.S. Navy Photo)*

connected each explosive charge to a main trunk line of detonating wire. When all was in readiness, the majority of the frogmen swam to safety.

Only two men remained behind. These two men waited until their comrades were out of harm's way. Then, acting on a prearranged smoke signal from a distant speedboat, they depressed the plunger on their compact electric detonator. As the electrical impulse traveled down the time-delay fuse, the two men swam furiously out toward sea, out toward their scheduled rendezvous with a pickup boat. The small craft, a retrieving loop dangling from its side, swooped down on the waiting men. The swimmers reached out for the loop and were jerked out of the water and onto the boat's decking.

And as they sped away from the island, the two courageous frogmen looked back toward the beach. Suddenly great geysers of sea water spurted toward the sky, and the thunder of the explosion caused the surface of the bay to erupt in boiling fury.

The job had been done. The path had been cleared. The stage was set. A continuous bombardment from the air and from the sea paved the way for the first landing crafts, filled with invading marines.

Subsequent battle statistics revealed the value of the ground-breaking work of the UDTs at Guam. For every casualty inflicted upon the Americans, ten enemy soldiers were killed. Vice Admiral W. L. Ainsworth, describing the Guam invasion in his official action report, summed it all up by saying, "This campaign was brilliantly planned and precisely executed."

However, more often than not, the courageous UDTs

did their tasks without praise, without credit. Since their very existence remained a closely guarded secret throughout the war, our own soldiers often failed to realize that the skin divers had paved the way for every major invasion.

Such was not the case, however, when those first Marines stormed onto Guam on the twentieth day of

Navy frogman, leaving an invasion site, grasps retrieving loop which dangles from the side of a high speed pick-up craft. The loop catapults the diver into the boat without requiring a decrease in speed. (U.S. Navy Photo)

July, 1944. As the leathernecks waded up onto the beach, they were greeted by a cheery, hand-painted sign, prominently displayed.

> *Welcome to Guam, U.S. Marines!*
> *USO—two blocks to the right.*
> *Underwater Demolition Team No. 4*

Following the end of World War II, many of our weapons were placed in mothballs and labeled "obsolete." This was not the case with the frogmen. Today's aqualung, coupled with other recent technological advances, has only increased our navy's emphasis on the underwater warrior.

Today, as in the past, the frogman must undergo a lengthy and extensive training period before he can "win his flippers." Two hundred physically fit young sailors journey every year to the Navy's Underwater Swimmer's School in Key West, Florida. During the first phase of their underwater education, the swimmers must master all the finer points of swimming with an aqualung.

But this is just the beginning. After qualifying as expert skin divers, the men are encouraged to continue their training in either one of two fields—UDT (Underwater Demolition Team) or EOD (Explosive Ordinance Disposal). Whichever course he selects, the student can be sure of only one thing—hard work, and plenty of it.

During a recent visit to the U. S. Naval School at Indian Head, Maryland, we followed a prospective EOD diver through a small portion of his seven and one half months of training. The trainee, used to the

A member of the Amphibious Force, U.S. Atlantic Fleet on a demolition mission. Note the package of explosives he carries. (*U.S. Navy Photo*)

clear, warm waters off Key West, must also master diving techniques under the worst possible conditions. Consequently his first dives carried him into the cold, muddied waters of the Potomac River.

Later we asked one young sailor to estimate the visibility in his new underwater classroom.

"It is approximately the same as you might expect to find in the stomach of a whale on a dark night," he reported solemnly.

The trainee soon learns to rely exclusively on his sense of touch, while wearing cumbersome, three fingered gloves. In the weeks that follow he learns to deactivate all modern forms of mine—contact mines, influence mines, torpedoes. He then advances to booby traps and land mines, hand grenades and bombs, and finally to the extremely complex field of nuclear missiles.

His final examination requires a steady hand and a backlog of classroom experience and practical knowledge. Working once again in the murky Potomac, he deactivates a variety of "live" mines, tows them to shore, and breaks them down into their component parts.

The would-be frogmen who select the UDT school undergo two months of arduous training under highly realistic combat conditions. "Hell Week," an aptly titled six-day period of dawn-to-dusk training, carries the trainee through icy waters, boggy swamps, and tangled jungles. Designed to separate the men from the boys, this arduous challenge effectively eliminates nearly fifty per cent of the candidates. Before he graduates from the Naval Amphibious School, the frogman must master over fifty separate subjects. And even after completing his course, the frogman returns periodically to the classroom and brushes up on the latest techniques.

The frogman's work, even in times of peace, can be extremely hazardous. His assignments are never easy. And his dives are often dives to danger. We discovered this during a recent conversation with one of our outstanding peacetime frogmen, Lieutenant Commander W. H. Hamilton, Jr.

A graduate of the United States Naval Academy in 1949, Commander Hamilton is a young man in his mid-thirties. His brief career has been outstanding in every respect. While serving with distinction during the Korean War, the youthful officer learned how to pilot every type of aircraft then used by the Navy.

When the conflict in Korea came to an end, he volunteered for the UDT training course. After graduating with honors, he went on to devise the first practical use of the helicopter as a hovering base of operations for an Underwater Demolition Team. Later named Executive Officer of the Underwater Swimmer's School, Commander Hamilton is now the leader of Underwater Demolition Unit II.

During our talk with the brilliant young officer, he shrugged off all our questions dealing with any possible danger he might have encountered as a frogman.

"This is pretty tame stuff really," he said. "We manage to strike up a nodding acquaintance with several barracuda and some friendly sharks. Our biggest excitement was recovering some cannon from a sunken British sloop. And, of course, we do participate in some interesting research projects."

This modest statement most certainly qualifies Commander Hamilton for understatement-of-the-year honors. He failed to mention that one of his "interesting research projects" was a little test designed to find out whether a pilot could be safely ejected from a downed airplane sinking rapidly into the ocean.

Aircraft manufacturers had theorized that a pilot equipped with an aqualung might possibly escape through the plane's canopy even after it had crashed into the sea. However, there was only one way to put this theory to the test. And that was actually to attempt an aqualung escape from a submerged airplane.

Unwilling to risk the lives of his men on such a dangerous project, Commander Hamilton volunteered to serve as the human guinea pig himself.

Consequently, one pleasantly warm morning not too long ago, he found himself seated behind the controls of a jet fighter plane exactly one hundred feet beneath the surface of the water. Fortunately the cockpit canopy opened. The test was a success. And the young officer performed the first human underwater ejection in this nation's history.

Commander Hamilton's official military record now carries a letter of commendation that notes: "Because of your efforts, more men will now have a chance to get out of a water crash alive and not be carried down with the airplane."

Commander Hamilton makes no claim to heroism. He is merely following in the tradition of the frogmen, the unsung heroes of today's navies. He is merely following the trail carved by Commander Crabb in the Mediterranean, by Underwater Demolition Team No. 4 at Guam, and by all the underwater warriors who habitually and willingly risk their lives for their fellow man.

5. Museum Beneath the Sea

PORT ROYAL, a beautiful, sun-drenched haven beside the Caribbean, was once known as the most evil city on the face of the earth. The notorious pirate Henry Morgan selected this idyllic spot for his headquarters. Ships anchored in the harbor displayed the skull and crossbones emblem with impunity. Professional plunderers and cutthroats roamed the narrow roads without fear of the law; Port Royal's only law was the survival of the fittest.

Then, shortly before noon one hot day in June, the entire city vanished.

Historians inevitably link Port Royal's disappearance with the destruction of two earlier evil cities described in the Old Testament: "Then the Lord rained in Sodom and Gomorrah brimstone and fire from the Lord out of heaven; and he overthrew those cities, and all the valley, and all the inhabitants of the cities, and what grew on the ground."

Although Port Royal did not suffer beneath a rain

of fire and brimstone, its destruction was equally complete, equally violent.

It began with an earthquake, an ominous tremor that shook the buildings and gave birth to an immense tidal wave. A wall of water, broad and all-engulfing, crashed over the town—drowning two thousand people, tumbling water-front taverns into the sea, uprooting trees and plants, forever burying Port Royal beneath the sparkling blue waters of the Caribbean.

As the years passed, time and tide completed the burial ceremonies. Silt and mud drifted over the sunken city. Seaweeds flourished in the main road. Tropical fish swam through decaying gambling halls. Octopuses set up housekeeping in the unused wine cellars.

Eventually the pirates were forced back into the pages of history. Merchant vessels and fishing boats once again sailed safely through the area. Port Royal, an underwater ghost town, was forgotten.

Not so long ago, however, a ship set sail from Key West, Florida. Its destination: Port Royal. It was a sleek white craft with the words *Sea Diver II* printed across its bow. Ninety-one feet in length, this vessel was going on a trip back into time, a voyage toward a city that the world had forgotten.

Built and equipped by Edwin Link of the Link Aviation Corporation, the *Sea Diver II* is operated under the guidance of the Smithsonian Institution. It carries a complete array of modern skin-diving equipment and a complex of electronic machinery used in archaeology, the science that investigates human history as revealed in the monuments and relics of ancient civilizations.

The scientists aboard the ship were not looking for

buried pirate treasure. Their sole interest was in the gathering of knowledge. They hoped to learn about life in the seventeenth century in Port Royal, the natural habitat of a dying species of man known as the pirate.

Anchoring directly above the sunken city, they discovered the water was constantly murky—as though nature intended to bury the wicked city forever beneath a muddy cloud. Since the visibility was never greater than ten feet, the first task was to draw a rough map of the underwater village.

As the scientists began to outline the scope of their work, they relied on many of the most delicate instruments used by underwater archaeologists. Magneto-makers and electronic metal detectors searched out the presence of metal beneath the mud. The sea scanner—a modern depth finder—was able to record the presence of old buildings and other obstructions still protruding from the sea floor.

After outlining the scope of their task, the explorers into the past began the tedious process of removing the blanket of sand that covered the city. The most determined of all the workers were Edwin Link and his wife, Marion. Along with the other skilled skin divers, these two pioneers in the field of underwater archaeology made many trips to the bottom with cleaning apparatus similar to the subsurface "vacuum cleaners" used by the SCUBA gold prospectors beneath the rivers of California.

One of the most valuable instruments was a jet hose that blasted streams of water against the silt and sand with terrific force. Another machine, a large version of the gold dredge, sucked away debris and filtered it through devices that would capture any small items of interest.

As the work continued, the archaeologists discovered an amazing fact: after nearly three centuries beneath the sea, much of Port Royal was still intact.

Proceeding more cautiously now, the scientists came upon their real treasure, the objects that would reveal how the pirates lived, what they ate, what they drank, how they furnished their homes—spoons and knives, coins of silver and gold, casks of soured wine. Some objects were brought to the surface by the air lift; others were carried up by the divers. Larger items were lifted by the ship's powerful cranes.

The results: several hundred well-preserved objects were recovered, cleansed, protected and preserved for future study and evaluation by the experts at the Smithsonian Institution.

One of the most prized objects recovered by the Links was an ancient brass pocket watch. The hands of the timepiece had fallen off and the metal parts were corroded. Scientists photographed the face of the watch beneath infrared lighting and discovered faint traces remaining to mark the position of the missing hands when the timepiece stopped operating. This enabled the archaeologists to determine the exact minute that Port Royal was destroyed—precisely twenty minutes before twelve.

Discovery is nothing new to the Links. Edwin Link is the inventor of the Link trainer and a pioneer in the world of modern aviation. His wife Marion, a former newspaper reporter, is the mother of two boys and an underwater archaeologist of many years' standing.

Five years ago the Links made one of their major discoveries off the coast of Haiti.

This search was to carry them back nearly five centuries, back to Christmas Eve of 1492. This was the year that Christopher Columbus piloted his three ships into the treacherous, reef-studded waters surrounding the island of Haiti. However, Columbus's flagship, the *Santa Maria*, never completed this journey. On the night before Christmas she piled up on a coral reef and sank.

Although Columbus was able to escape with his life, the ship was not so fortunate. It lay forgotten beneath the sea—forgotten, that is, until the Links took up the search. Before embarking on this undertaking, they spent two years collecting all available information about Columbus and his route through the harbor. After consulting all known authorities, they went so far as to have the Italian explorer's log translated into English.

Then the search began.

The Links spent many days patrolling the harbor in a small glass-bottomed boat known as the *Reef Diver*. During the next few weeks the Links turned up several old anchors, but all were proven to be of relatively recent construction.

Beset by rough seas, hampered by the local authorities, bruised and battered by the long and unrewarding search, the Links were preparing to call it a day. Even the diving had become an arduous chore. Edwin had suffered a broken toe, and his wife, bandages covering her bruised rib cage, had difficulty moving her right arm. As their hunt neared its end, the Links went out on one last wild-goose chase.

The last ship they were to examine turned out to be another false alarm, a craft that had probably gone to its watery grave only several decades ago. As Marion Link headed toward the surface to relay the bad news to her injured husband, she suddenly noticed another object lying several yards from the recent wreck. It was an anchor, a small anchor of simple design.

Reporting her discovery to her husband, Marion suggested quite casually that he might want to take a look at it. Although he had seen too many anchors to hold out much hope for this one, Edwin Link hobbled to the side of the ship and climbed down the ladder to the water. Within five minutes he was back at the ship.

"I think we've got it," he announced. "It looks like the real McCoy."

The ancient, coral-covered anchor was lifted onto the main ship, and the scientific investigation began. The anchor was first measured, and turned out to be seventy-eight inches long and fifty-two inches in width—the same size as the anchors used in Columbus's era. Working with hammer and file, Link then began the task of stripping the layers of coral from the iron base. It was then seen that the anchor had been hand made and welded, unlike the cast-iron products of later years.

Scientific examination proved beyond a doubt that it had, indeed, come from Columbus's era. It was, in all probability, the anchor from the doomed *Santa Maria*.

Years of study. Months of preparation. Weeks of hard work. And then—after all the expense, after all the arduous labor—one rusting anchor.

Why would anyone take such great trouble with such apparently unrewarding results? The answer to this riddle lies in the basic nature of archaeology, a science that values the search for knowledge above the search for any other form of treasure.

Archaeology is the scientific study of ancient man's entire way of life. In a vital and dramatic sense it is an extension of history. The historian is primarily interested in Caesar's conquests; the archaeologist is more concerned with Caesar's subjects—the clothes they wore, the food they ate, the tools they used, the gods they worshiped.

Underwater archaeology—the exploration of the vast museum beneath the sea—began in 1907 when a Greek helmet diver first noticed a series of strange mounds on the floor of the Mediterranean. Arranged

Anchor of a wrecked ancient Roman ship discovered by skin diving archaeologists in the Mediterranean.

in a regular pattern, the formations were located three miles off the Tunisian port of Mahdia.

Scraping aside some of the mud, the helmet divers uncovered enormous marble columns—over sixty of them. And beneath the columns could be seen the beginnings of an ancient, round-bottomed ship.

The work went slowly. Since the aqualung had not yet been invented, the divers had to work in awkward, helmeted diving suits, their air supplied through a hose from their ship. While they worked, they constantly had to combat a powerful current; with every step they kicked up clouds of blinding silt.

During the next six years the divers returned to Mahdia on five different excursions. Working at a depth of twenty fathoms, they lifted and removed the marble columns. Then they began to remove many of the normal shipboard appliances—cooking pots, lamps, brass furnishings, lead anchors.

Breaking into the ship's hold, they discovered a veritable museum of ancient art works—statues, urns, vases, wine jugs—enough material to fill many rooms of Tunis's Bardo Museum.

Each item became a piece in a puzzle. The archaeologist's task is to fit those pieces together and to create an accurate portrait of an ancient man and an entire civilization. To accomplish this, he must ask three basic questions about each scrap of evidence: Why was it made? When was it made? Who made it?

It would be impossible to detail all the information that was discovered at this one site.

From the size and shape of the ship, the archaeologist realizes that it was built by the Romans during the first

Divers examining objects recovered from what is believed to be the *Sea Venture*, a sailing ship which sank off Bermuda in the early 17th century. (*Wide World Photos*)

century before Christ. Awkward of construction, slow of speed, overloaded with cargo, the ship reveals that the Romans were not able to master the sea with the skill of their neighbors, the Greeks and Phoenicians.

From the statues, the archaeologist is able to learn much about the technique and training of the ancient Roman artists. From the form of the art, he discovers much new information about the gods of ancient man.

The amphorae, large earthen jugs used to carry oil and wine, tell another tale. The markings and shaping of each urn reveal where and when it was manufactured. Fragments of metal—nails and candle holders—reveal many vital factors about the state of Roman industry.

This was the first great underwater archaeological find.

Since the invention of the aqualung there have been many other extremely valuable discoveries. A Chicago treasure hunter recently found an entire city buried beneath the surface of Lake Titicaca. Experts feel he may have stumbled upon the very center of the ancient Incan civilization. Other amateur skin divers have uncovered nearly a hundred Greco-Roman ships buried beneath the steadily rising waters of the Mediterranean.

There are many other sites waiting for the skin-diving archaeologist. There are entire cities lying beneath water bordering Greece and Yugoslavia. And eventually some enterprising skin diver may discover the fabled Atlantis, the lost continent which many historians feel was the birthplace of all civilization.

Unfortunately, most of the major discoveries of the past decade have been made by amateur skin divers with little knowledge of archaeology. And in this case a little knowledge can most definitely be a dangerous thing.

During our trip along the Riviera we discovered a thriving black market in objects that had been looted from the holds of ancient ships. An amphora manufactured by the Greeks during Christ's lifetime could be purchased for about eighty dollars.

The skin divers who have carelessly plundered sunken

ships are often guilty of ruining the vessel for the scientist. Archaeologists—Johnnies-come-lately to the world of SCUBA—must be content with only leftovers, with the picked carcass of the once-proud sailing vessel.

The archaeologist is traditionally caricatured as a bearded professor wearing a pith helmet and walking across a sandy desert with a magnifying glass in his hand. In reality he must be a man of great education. He must be skilled in many languages, both living and dead. He must study many civilizations, both modern and ancient. He must pry into many worlds, both old and new.

There is no short cut to his knowledge. And since most skin divers know little about ancient history, a concentrated effort is now being made to interest archaeologists in skin diving. It has been discovered, however, that while you can lead an archaeologist to water, you cannot always make him dive.

One solution to this problem was offered several years ago by Captain Jacques-Yves Cousteau, "the father of the aqualung." An ancient cargo ship had been discovered twenty fathoms beneath the water off the port of Marseilles. Captain Cousteau explored the site with a team consisting of both expert skin divers and skilled archaeologists.

While the divers probed the entombed ship and carried away many thousands of valuable objects, the scientists remained aboard the oceanographic ship, *Calypso*. They participated in the search without even getting their toes wet.

The archaeologists sat in a comfortable cabin, smoked cigars, and watched television. The television program they watched was neither a Western nor a mystery. It

was a closed-circuit telecast—linked by cable to a portable camera on the bottom of the sea—of the divers at
work. By relaying instructions and advice through an
underwater loud-speaker system, the scientists were
able to direct every step of the most successful underwater archaeological expedition in history.

6. Bring 'em Back Alive

WE AWAKENED two hours before sunrise and unhitched our power launch from its offshore moorings. There was no breeze and the Florida seas were calm. No visible horizon separated the predawn skies and the dark ocean; ahead we could see only night. Our boat's headlight glanced aimlessly off the placid swells and dissolved in the distance.

"It'll be a fine day," Cappy Anson predicted, "a fine day for the hunt."

Chewing the stem of an unlit pipe, the twenty-three-year-old hunter followed a southerly course toward the Florida Keys. Unlike other skin-diving hunters, Cappy Anson used no spear gun in his search for rare and exotic fish. Just as Frank Buck had sought to trap jungle animals without injuring them, Cappy Anson also aimed to "bring 'em back alive."

As we rounded the tip of the Florida peninsula, Cappy changed direction, heading west toward the Gulf of Mexico. The skies behind us lightened and the May sun

Among the wonders of the deep are the many varieties of coral. Skin diver is wearing modern "oranasal breathing mask" that requires no mouthpiece.

quickly shredded the fragments of mist draped over the water.

"Where are we heading, Cappy?"

"To my favorite hunting spot," he replied. "To the coral reefs."

This was our first visit to the reefs, ledges of living coral that follow the Florida shore line from south of Miami to Tortuga Island. Constructed by millions of almost microscopically tiny animals, the reefs sometimes rest ten fathoms beneath the surface, and other times jut up to form small islands. Hundreds of ships, ranging

from ancient Spanish galleons to today's modern power
boats, have been splintered against these deceptive reefs.

By midmorning we had arrived at the cluster of irreg-
ular islands known as the Ragged Keys. Cappy piloted
the boat to the sheltered side of the islands and anchored
in a shallow inlet bordered by an uninhabited beach.
About fifteen feet of brilliant blue water lay above
the reefs at this point. The water, warmed by the Gulf
Stream, registered a surface temperature of seventy-
nine degrees.

After testing our aqualungs, we sat in the boat and
listened to Cappy's final instructions.

"There's no telling what we'll find down there," he
said. "There may be some sharks or a barracuda or two.
And we generally see a moray eel hanging around the
door to his cave. But don't worry—if you don't bother
them, they won't bother you."

We quickly assured Cappy that we had not the
slightest intention of bothering them.

"Fine," he smiled. "Just don't touch any fish with
spines. In fact you'd better not touch any fish without
first asking me. Watch where you put your feet—the
yellow fire coral will sting like poison ivy. And so will
the jellyfish. Just stay close to me and there'll be no
trouble."

"What fish are you hunting today?"

"The lionfish," he said. "These are fairly rare, and
each specimen should net us about a hundred dollars."

"A hundred dollars!" we commented. "That seems
like a lot of money to spend on just one fish."

"Well, there *is* one little catch," he said. "The lionfish belongs to the family of scorpion fish. His sharp

dorsal fins can slice through your hand as though it were butter.

"But that's not the worst of it," he continued. "Those spines are hollow and filled with poison. Just one drop of that poison is enough to kill a man. And, from what I hear, it's not a pretty way to die."

"Sounds like fun."

"Oh, it will be," Cappy assured us. "Just remember to stay away from the fins. You should handle the lionfish with the same respect you'd give to a rattlesnake."

After testing our aqualungs, we climbed down the ladder and entered the tepid water. Our only weapon against the poisonous lionfish was a small net, similar to the type used by butterfly hunters.

Our first impression was one of great clarity. The summer sun reflected against the white sand and illuminated the entire undersea world. Objects over a hundred feet away could be seen with no difficulty.

As we approached the reef itself, we were next impressed by the wide range of colors. It seemed painted with pastel shades of red and yellow and violet.

Closer inspection revealed that the reef was an immense underwater city. Millions of tiny animals had labored for centuries to construct this submarine metropolis. The primary builder was a tiny transparent animal known as the coral polyp. Each polyp is able to secrete calcium carbonate to construct a tiny protective shell of limestone around itself. Countless of these cuplike structures had banded together in the form of colonies.

The colonies—housing developments in the underwater city—took many different architectural forms.

Strange and beautiful coral formations. *(U.S. Navy Photo)*

Some resembled branches and bushes. Others jutted up like the antlers of an enormous elk. We saw several colonies of coral that resembled the human brain.

The main structure of the reef, a solid core of limestone, was the graveyard for past generations of coral polyps. Only the animals on the top and side surfaces of the reef were still alive. And these continued to grow and multiply, increasing the size of the reef about one inch every year.

Other animals lived on the top of the reef. We saw lobster, starfish, colorful sponges, and those black pincushions known as sea urchins.

Cappy interrupted our study of the reef by signaling us to move on with the hunt. Drifting behind him, we turned our attention to the fish. We immediately understood why these fish were sought and prized by aquariums and private collectors everywhere.

Never before had we seen such colors as these. Brilliant stripes, vivid polka dots—as though the fish had been hand-painted by an artist with a gaudy sense of color and a bizarre sense of humor. Glittering like jewels, patterned after exotic butterflies, these fish made the inhabitants of other seas seem drab and lackluster in comparison. Science has never been able to explain fully the intoxicating range of colors adorning coral-reef fish. It is certainly not for purposes of camouflage; the fish could not have been more noticeable if each had carried a miniature neon advertisement.

Many varieties seemed to exist in close quarters. A lonely demoiselle fish, brilliant in her gown of iridescent blue, studied our approach with interest. Three big-eyed squirrelfish, bright orange with yellow-tipped fins, turned their backs on us and meandered away with slow dignity. A cluster of green dwarf wrasses fluttered away like surprised starlings. A family of tiny comical sea horses, clinging to coral branches with their tails, took absolutely no notice of us.

But we saw no sign of the lionfish.

Checking our air supply, we discovered that we had been below for nearly half an hour. Turning regretfully away from the reef, we paddled back toward the boat, rising slowly toward the surface as we went. After climbing aboard, we rested for a few moments.

"There were so many fish down there," we said.

"How do you know which one is a lionfish?"

"There's no mistaking a lionfish," Cappy said. "Just look for an underwater nightmare."

"An underwater nightmare?"

"You'll understand when—and if—we find one," he said. "Meanwhile, we'll concentrate on some other varieties. While we're resting, we might as well try some new territory."

Lifting anchor, Cappy started his powerful twin outboard motors. Cruising at the slowest possible speed, we followed the reef and studied the submarine terrain through a plate-glass window constructed in the boat's bottom. The window gave us a clear view downward, serving much the same purpose as the diver's face mask.

Our second dive turned up no creature that remotely resembled an "underwater nightmare." Most of the fish seemed carved from dreams of a decidedly pleasant nature. Indicating one group of particularly exotic fish, Cappy held up his underwater slate and scribbled the word "angel."

These fish—the queen angelfish—were approximately two feet in length. Blue and yellow of contrasting shades, they had graceful dorsal and anal fins flowing from them like trails of liquid gold.

Following Cappy's lead, we approached them cautiously, slowly. After he had netted one, we each followed suit. Returning to the boat with our prizes, we were quite proud of the ease with which we had landed them. Much to our chagrin, Cappy quickly rejected our offerings and returned them to the sea. As he deposited his specimen in one of the boat's specially constructed salt-water tanks, he explained his action.

"Don't feel bad," he said. "The queen angelfish looks peaceful enough, but two of them confined to the same tank will turn on each other. When they were through ripping each other apart with their sharp gill spikes, we wouldn't have enough left for bait."

On subsequent excursions below we fared much better. On one trip we brought in several jewelfish, valued at almost thirty dollars each. On the next trip we caught our first glimpse of the Portuguese man-of-war, one of the deadliest jellyfish known to man.

Seen from the surface, the man-of-war appeared relatively harmless. It floated along like a partially inflated balloon topped by a small sail-like structure. However, seen from the skin diver's viewpoint, it takes on a decidedly different appearance. Long stingers—gleaming, luminescent red and green—dangled a full ten feet beneath the creature's floating cap. These stingers have caused untold pain to unwary skin divers and careless fish.

Knowing this, we were surprised to discover several small fish swimming safely through the maze of tentacles. Apparently unbothered by the man-of-war's poison, the tiny silver-and-blue rudder fish seemed to thrive in their ominous surroundings. Cappy motioned us back and signaled that he was going to try to snare some of the rudder fish.

He circled the giant jellyfish cautiously, keeping just out of reach of the protective curtains of poisonous arms. Then in a single, rapid motion he thrust his net into the center of the mass.

At first it looked as though he had succeeded in his quest. Retreating from the Portuguese man-of-war, he

A crab is an uninvited guest as diver serves birthday cake to a porpoise at an underwater party. (*Wide World Photos*)

supported two of the small fish in his net. Then when he appeared to be free and clear, he suddenly dropped his catch and clutched his right arm.

We rushed to Cappy's side and eased him back toward the boat. However, before ascending to the surface, Cappy scooped up a handful of white sand from the bottom. Once aboard the boat, he began furiously to massage his right forearm with the sand.

"I'll be all right," he muttered. "This isn't a bad sting. I'll be all right."

It may not have been a bad sting, but the pain showed in Cappy Anson's youthful face. After scraping off any of the tentacles that might still be clinging to his arm, he tilted a fuel container and splashed the gasoline over his infected arm. Either gasoline or alcohol will help kill any of the remaining nematocysts—tiny stinging cells that remain imbedded in the flesh.

"You can't see them," Cappy said, "but you sure can feel them."

Moments later the pain had ceased and only a narrow strip of pink skin remained to remind us of Cappy's brief but painful encounter with the Portuguese man-of-war. During the remainder of the day we concentrated on relatively harmless fish—the demoiselles and cardinals and parrotfish. Our enthusiasm mounted with each trip, and we soon forgot about our original prey—the rare and dangerous lionfish.

Only one other unfortunate incident marred the hunt. That occurred when we discovered a strange green fish with arms, lurking among the seaweed. This animal, apparently a cross between a frog and a fish, was in the process of dining when we first saw him.

The sargassum fish snared his meal in a most unusual manner. He dangled a small tab from his dorsal fin in much the same way that a fisherman dangles a baited hook in the water. Smaller fish approaching the tab were promptly added to the menu.

We netted the sargassum fish and carried him to the surface. Cappy, preparing to climb back into the water, smiled his approval.

"Good work," he said. "He's quite rare. He'll bring a good price on the mainland."

After depositing the sargassum fish in the tank inhabited by demoiselles, we returned to the water and joined Cappy on the reef. On our next trip back to the boat we discovered that the three demoiselles had mysteriously disappeared. Only our sargassum remained in the tank.

"I should have warned you," Cappy said. "The sargassum has got a stomach that stretches like a rubber band. He'll eat his own weight in fish and then ask for a second helping."

"You mean he managed to eat those other fish that quickly?"

"That was just an appetizer for the sargassum," Cappy said. "An expensive appetizer—about sixty dollars' worth. I think our fat friend there will have a private compartment for the rest of the trip."

As our long day of hunting neared its end, we discovered a most unusual rock nestled among the seaweed. It seemed to carry many unusual colors—vivid markings set against a background of pink. Cappy, swimming ahead of us, did not notice the stone. However, we lowered ourselves for a closer look.

As we studied it, the strange rock suddenly moved.

The seaweed also moved. Then we realized that the "seaweed" was, in reality, attached to the fish. The dermal flaps, loose pieces of skin, swayed gently in the water.

Cappy, turning back, also saw our find and immediately placed his hand across his throat, giving the skin diver's signal for danger. It was then that we realized that we had finally discovered the dreaded lionfish. And at the same time, the lionfish discovered us.

As he rose to greet us, we remembered Cappy's warning to treat it with all the respect we would accord a rattlesnake. We froze. The absence of air bubbles revealed that we were both holding our breath.

Cappy's description of the "underwater nightmare" had been quite accurate. The fish looked like a pint-sized refugee from the era of the dinosaur. Yellows, browns, and pinks formed a frightening pattern over the ugly fish's mottled skin.

Our eyes never left the dorsal fins—the poison-carrying spikes protruding prominently from his back. The fish demonstrated neither fear nor aggression. He studied us with unintelligent, lidless eyes.

Cappy, approaching us all too slowly, waited no longer. With one quick sweep of his hand net, he ended the hunt on a happy note. The lionfish twisted and turned, but could not escape from the trap. Then, as though he realized the futility of his struggle, he gave up the fight.

Only then did the bubbles flow again from our aqualungs. Only then did we again breathe easily.

"Good work," Cappy congratulated us as he housed the lionfish in the tank next to the sargassum. "That was quite brave of you. There aren't many divers who would go that close to a lionfish.

We didn't bother to correct his faulty impression.

"What kept you?" we asked. "We thought you'd never come to get him."

"I didn't want to scare him away," he explained. "I knew he wouldn't attack you. He was probably just curious. They may look ferocious, but they actually make quite nice pets. Some owners claim that they can train the lionfish to eat right out of their hands."

As we headed back with our catch, we found that the work of the "live hunter" does not end with the hunt. Great care has to be taken to avoid rough water. Ironically enough, the fish will get seasick if there's too much motion.

Once we were ashore, we had to package the fish for shipment. They were placed in a plastic bag filled with ocean water that had been collected on the incoming tide. To keep the water "fresh" for a twenty-four-hour period, we then inserted a tube leading to a cylinder of compressed oxygen and inflated the bag. This was then placed in a second bag made of the same heavy plastic and then deposited in a box labeled "Live Fish." The containers were rushed to a nearby airport so that they could be flown to collectors as far away as Iowa.

Cappy Anson is just one of many skin divers who enjoy all the excitement of underwater hunting without having to kill their prey. We have seen porpoises captured with a hypodermic spear gun that injected a strong tranquilizer into their blood streams. And a visit to Miami's Seaquarium showed us some of the accomplishments of Captain William Gray, the most famous of all "live hunters." Captain Gray is a man who has lassoed sharks, grappled with porpoises, and netted whales.

One of the most unusual SCUBA hunts on record was undertaken by Harry Goodridge, a skin diver who lives in Rockport, Maine. Last summer, while swimming in the chill waters of Penobscot Bay, Harry met a baby seal. The seal, thoroughly frightened, turned tail and swam away. Harry followed.

At first it was no contest. A seal—even a baby seal—can easily outswim a man. However, Harry had the advantage of endurance. When the small animal was finally forced to surface for air, Harry followed him and simply grabbed him beneath the flippers. The seal, thoroughly tuckered out, allowed himself to be carried ashore by the skin diver.

As a result, Harry Goodridge has the most unusual pet in the town of Rockport. The seal, subsequently dubbed Basil, settled down happily in his new living quarters—a doghouse built in Harry's back yard. He only returns to the ocean when his master goes on one of his frequent skin-diving trips.

Recently, however, Basil showed signs of loneliness. And one morning he waddled off to the water's edge by himself. When he came home that evening, Basil brought a friend with him—Alvin, another seal who soon learned to enjoy the easy living found in Harry Goodrich's back yard.

"So far, so good," Harry Goodrich said recently. "But I'm afraid that if this keeps up, we'll have to add another wing to our doghouse."

7. Picture of Danger

THE SKIN DIVER peered cautiously through a clearing in the woods. The sandy cove seemed deserted. Convinced that the coast was clear, the muscular young man left the safety of the tropical underbrush and walked out onto the open beach.

An underwater trouble shooter, this skin diver was employed by a small South American country. His mission was a particularly dangerous one: to recover the national treasure concealed off the Bahamas by the recently unseated dictator. It was assumed that the treasure would be guarded.

Wading slowly out into the translucent waters, the diver gripped his aqualung mouthpiece firmly and assumed a horizontal position. He submerged without so much as a splash to mark his point of entry.

His every movement showed him to be an expert skin diver. There was no needless motion, no wasted energy. Keeping his arms pinned to his sides, he propelled himself with a slow but powerful flutter kick. To conserve his supply of compressed air, the swimmer rationed himself to one breath for every eight kicks.

He paused every few moments to glance in all directions. He was not being followed. His only companions were the colorful fish and plants of the tropical coral reef.

Ahead of him, apparently unprotected, was the object of his search. The nail-studded trunk sat in the center of an exposed coral plateau. It had barely settled on the sea floor, and its metal surface was free of plant life.

Inserting a pry bar into the trunk's lock, the diver started to pry it open. As he concentrated all his strength on the task, he momentarily relaxed his guard. He failed to notice a second arrival—another SCUBA diver, swimming toward him with an unsheathed knife in his right hand.

The lock resisted his efforts for several more moments and then finally snapped. The diver raised the lid of the trunk and looked in. It was filled with gold bars, stolen from the small country's treasury.

As he prepared to surface to signal a waiting speedboat, the diver suddenly sensed the presence of danger. He wheeled around. Coming at him was a diver in a black suit, with a glinting knife in his outstretched hand.

This marked the beginning of a vicious underwater fight. The two men, both wearing aqualungs, twisted and turned in mortal combat. They rolled over on the sea floor, kicking up clouds of sand. The unknown attacker, unable to draw blood with his knife, managed to slash the tube carrying air from the cylinder to the mouthpiece.

The first diver countered by swinging his pry bar

against his enemy's arm. Pain and surprise flickered through the other diver's eyes as his right arm went limp. The knife fell from his useless fingers.

As he retrieved the weapon, the victor began to feel the need for air. Holding the blade against his opponent's threat, he forced the second man to relinquish his mouthpiece. Thereafter using the buddy breathing system—two men sharing the same air supply—they rose slowly toward the surface. The waiting speedboat raced to the rescue.

There was still no time to spare. Rifle shots from the adjacent shore line kicked up miniature geysers of water near the boat. After slipping into another aqualung, the diver descended once again, this time to attach a winch cable to the sunken treasure. As the machinery lifted the trunk into the small boat, the diver joined his companions on the surface. The rifle bullets ripped through the side of the vessel as it raced quickly from the area.

We watched this drama as it unfolded one warm morning in May.

And several weeks later we watched it again—this time seated comfortably before our television set. For this was one installment of the popular skin-diving adventure series, "Sea Hunt."

After the filming of the underwater fight, we spoke to Lloyd Bridges, the star of the television series and an expert skin diver in his own right. After the strenuous episode with the diver in the black suit, Mr. Bridges was not even breathing heavily. We asked him whether he ever encountered any actual danger during the filming of his adventures.

Diver with equipment for underwater photography. (*U.S. Navy Photo*)

"No, not really," he replied. "The only ones around here who take chances are the cameramen. They'll do anything, go anywhere, just for a good picture."

During the next few months we learned to appreciate the truth behind Lloyd Bridges's words. We have seen underwater photographers casually bump their camera housing units against the snout of a shark. We have seen them lure sharks to an area with scraps of bait, then calmly enter the bloodied water to photograph the beasts during the insane frenzy of "mob feeding."

A French biologist, Dr. Louis Bouton, made the first successful underwater photographs during the 1890s. Protecting his camera in a bulky copper box, using metal plates instead of standard film and igniting the sea bottom with powdered magnesium, Dr. Bouton worked under the most primitive conditions and still managed to produce photographs of relatively high quality.

Not until 1917 was a metal camera unit with outside controls developed. And precisely one decade later the first color pictures and the first motion pictures were taken beneath the surface.

Despite these advances, underwater photography remained in the experimental stages until just a few years ago. The problems were many; the solutions, few.

Light—the basic ingredient for any photograph—presented the biggest single stumbling block. Hazy water, a choppy surface, an overcast sky—these unpredictable factors all tend to reduce the supply of underwater light.

Moreover, as the cameraman descends, the light diminishes and the colors begin to disappear. Red vanishes at a depth of about thirty feet. Then orange, then yellow—until, one by one, all the rays of the spectrum are filtered out of existence. Deep-swimming skin divers who suffer minor cuts are often startled to discover that their blood seems tinted a very aristocratic shade of blue: at the lower depths the diver encounters a world composed entirely of blues and greens. Below a thousand feet all light rays have been cut off by the thick blanket of water, and eternal night covers all.

These obstacles have been overcome through the

technical advances of recent years. And today anyone able to push a button can learn to take striking underwater photos. We discovered this during our trips to the coral reefs rimming the Florida Keys. This area of clear water and colorful fish is a mecca for the subsurface cameraman.

Our guide and teacher was Jason McPhee, a commercial photographer in Miami for over two decades. In the past McPhee was content to photograph dimpled babies, cake-cutting newlyweds, graduating high school seniors, and family pets. Eight years ago he tried on his first aqualung. Since that moment his life has undergone several radical changes.

He is still slight of build, balding, conservative in dress and speech. Although he resembles a modest college professor, he has earned a reputation as one of the most fearless of the underwater cameramen.

He has photographed sharks and crocodiles, whales, and the vicious little South American piranha fish.

He is one man who will "do anything, go anywhere, just for a good picture."

Last May he received an assignment from a national magazine. The request was for a series of close-up pictures of the great barracuda, "preferably one exceeding six feet in length."

Jason invited us to accompany him so that we might observe the underwater cameraman in his natural habitat. Although we readily agreed, we had some misgivings. Authenticated records of barracuda attacking skin divers are rare. However, most experienced divers claim to prefer the company of a shark to that of a barracuda.

A slender, silvery fish with sharp teeth, the great

barracuda will strike an object at a speed greater than thirty miles an hour. Moreover, its maneuverability and high-speed accuracy far exceed that of a shark. The barracuda, like most other fish, is attracted by bright and sparkling objects. Unlike most other fish, however, it has been known to lunge for a diver's foot or even his aqualung in the confusion of murky water.

Our destination was the Key Largo Coral Reef Preserve, the world's first underwater national park. This reef, located three miles off the tip of the Florida peninsula, is a spawning ground for many different varieties of tropical fish. However, until recently it looked as though the reef might be ruined completely by commercial shell fishermen who regularly invaded the area with barges carrying dynamite and power hoists. In their search for rare shells and corals, these men would blast apart entire sections of reef.

In an eleventh-hour effort to conserve the fish and plant life, the federal government in 1960 made the area a public reservation. And today the commercial fishermen as well as spearfishing skin divers are banned from the reef. In their place have come the skin-diving tourists, sight-seers, and underwater cameramen.

Upon our arrival at the reef, we could fully appreciate the government's wisdom. The Key Largo Coral Reef Preserve is only twenty miles long and four miles wide. In this compact area nearly fifty different types of coral flourish.

Before undertaking our search for the great barracuda, Jason offered us a few technical pointers.

"We should get some good shots," he said. "The sun is bright and the water is calm. We'll have plenty of

Skin-diving photographer takes snapshot of coral formations formed on a sunken vessel.

light. However, if you've never taken pictures down below before, you may have to change your style somewhat. Try to get as close to your subject as possible— the wide-angle F 3.5 lens will help to cut down on the haze, but it can't do the entire job. You have to do your part."

"The water doesn't look hazy," we pointed out.

"Not to the eye," he said. "However, the eye sees things more clearly than the camera can. The camera lens will discover haze that the eye sees right through. That's why we'll use a fast film, one that will give us the greatest possible contrast. We'll also use a wide shutter opening and the fastest possible lens to assure clarity in details. I'd advise you to stick with a speed of about one-hundredth of a second. Since I'll be employing artificial lighting, I'll try for about a five-hundredth of a second."

"It sounds as though the equipment does all the work."

"Not at all," he smiled. "The most important part of any camera is the man behind it. Here it will be doubly important to hold the camera steady and to make sure that your focus is accurate. Also, try not to shoot down at the fish or you'll lose all sense of depth in your picture. And one last tip: don't be afraid of shadows. If portions of the picture are dark, it will provide better contrast for your main subject."

After absorbing these basic rules, we were introduced to our equipment. We were pleased to learn that the emphasis was on light-weight compactness and on simplicity of operation.

The most important item, of course, was the camera

itself. We were given 35-mm. box cameras that were able to shoot thirty-six different photographs before it would become necessary to surface for reloading. Since there might not be time for complicated adjustments, the camera used a simple level device instead of the traditional knob for advancing the roll of film after taking a shot. Jason's camera even went one step farther: a battery-powered electric mechanism automatically advanced the film after the shutter was tripped.

The cameras were protected from the water by housing units—simple, homemade boxes that Jason had built for a cost of less than fifteen dollars. The material used was a rigid, transparent plastic of half-inch thickness. Another popular model looks like a plastic balloon, and the cameraman is able to operate the controls by feeling through the pliable material.

Whatever its appearance, the housing unit must fill four basic requirements. It must be absolutely watertight. It must be sturdy enough to withstand the pressure of deep water. It must enable the skin diver to manipulate conveniently all the necessary levers. Finally, since the window shielding the camera lens acts as a second lens, it should equal the quality of optically ground plate glass.

Attached to the housing units were light meters—the devices used by all photographers to measure the amount of available light. Most underwater cameramen prefer the modern photoelectric light meter with direct reading apparatus. When using the meter, the skin diver must take care to avoid surface glare and sudden changes in lighting. The proper procedure is to take the reading halfway between the subject and the camera, with the light meter held at an angle toward the sea floor.

Another useful attachment to most submarine cameras is a lens filter. Some filters are effectively used to eliminate the blues that dominate the depths. However, we used a polarizing filter to cut down the glare in the shallower waters.

Since the water was quite bright, we had no need for flash apparatus. However, like most commercial cameramen, Jason McPhee carried his own supply of artificial light with him at all times. Although underwater lighting has come a long way since the days of exploding magnesium, it can still be a dangerous business in the hands of an amateur. Ordinary equipment—either the electronic flash or the standard clear flash bulb—must be carefully insulated by an expert. Moreover, some bulbs have a tendency to explode without warning in deep water.

Jason avoided these hazards with a modern piece of equipment that is rapidly gaining favor with most SCUBA photographers. His lighting supply—battery-powered flood lamps—was encaged with his camera in a torpedo-shaped cylinder. A distant miniature relative of the one-man submarine, this sleek underwater bullet added power and speed, enabling Jason to cover wide territory.

Since we could not hope to keep up with him, we contented ourselves with photographing the exotic corals and sponges that abounded everywhere. Jason returned periodically to check our progress, and surfaced to reload his camera and replace his air tanks, to go off once again in search of the barracuda.

On one of his return trips we noticed that he had

reduced his speed to a snail's pace. We also noticed that he had a companion. Sneaking along behind him, lurking just beneath the surface, was the streamlined form of the great barracuda. Apparently unconcerned, Jason drifted slowly past a shadowy break in the reef. The barracuda's coloring changed instantaneously from silver to black, camouflaging him perfectly against the dark background.

Believing that Jason must be unaware of the danger, we signaled him frantically by slicing our hands across our throats—the traditional skin diver's warning for danger. Much to our surprise, Jason replied by linking his right thumb and first finger to form a circle that is translated as "the situation is well in hand" in underwater sign language.

We knew enough about the barracuda to question Jason McPhee's sanity. The barracuda has been known to attack whether it is hungry or not. And when it goes for its prey, there is no chance to escape. Defenses against sharks—splashing, shouting, bumping his snout with pole or camera—are just minor annoyances to the barracuda.

As Jason decreased his speed, the barracuda closed the gap that separated them. As the great fish received a closer look at this strange creature known as a skin diver, he seemed to be in an ideal position to make a tasty snack of our friend.

It was then that Jason made his move. Taking care not to splash, he revolved slowly and directed his camera into the barracuda's yawning mouth. The fish, unafraid, stared at Jason with mild interest and then haughtily turned his back on the interloper and swam away.

Before he left, Jason had managed to capture two dozen close-up portraits of the fish.

As we joined Jason in the cockpit of the boat, he modestly shrugged off our words of praise.

"There was no danger," he informed us. "I was watching him in my rearview mirror."

For the first time we noticed that Jason had, indeed, attached a small metal rearview mirror to his power unit. However, we were still not convinced. Since a skin diver could never outrun a barracuda, it wouldn't make much difference whether he saw the fish coming or not.

"True enough," Jason replied. "However, a barracuda won't attack a man without provocation. Even when they've been wounded, they'll give you warning. This is the only fish I know that completely loses his temper. When he's angry, he begins to shake and shudder. His tail snaps back and forth like a rattlesnake's. When he opens his mouth, that's the time to start saying your prayers."

We asked Jason how he knew so much about an attacking barracuda. He answered our question by pointing to a white-rimmed red scar on his left calf.

"Last year I was trying to photograph one that had been speared," he explained. "He lost his temper somewhat. However, we did manage to get some excellent pictures."

Our excursion and our photographs came to a happy ending in the serenity of the darkroom. To increase the contrast on our finished prints, Jason allowed the negatives to remain in the developing chemical slightly longer than the prescribed amount of time. The prints themselves were made on highly sensitive photographic paper. Jason's photographs of the barracuda were fine enough to gladden the heart of any magazine editor. And surprisingly enough our own first efforts reproduced with vivid clarity.

By using modern equipment and following Jason's simple instructions, any skin diver can manage to produce fine portraits of the underwater world.

And this practice is not limited exclusively to photographers. During our travels we met quite a few skin divers who carry oil paints and stiff white cardboard and actually paint the submarine landscape.

However, the most accurate pictures of Neptune's kingdom are still made by the underwater cameraman. The development of inexpensive underwater equipment has opened vast new areas to the eye of the camera. And most important of all has been the technical revolution caused by television.

Experimental underwater television began in 1947, when United States scientists used closed-circuit television to examine nuclear tests off Bikini. Four years later the British used the same apparatus to examine a submarine that had sunk nearly three hundred feet below the surface of the English Channel.

However, not until the year 1957 did the underwater television camera receive its acid test. The Tennessee Valley Authority has always relied upon helmeted divers to inspect its great series of dams. However, the visibility was so poor that the divers had to check for cracks and other signs of erosion by running their fingers over the concrete surface of the dam.

The test was a simple one. A compact television camera was to be lowered one hundred feet beneath the waters of Wheeler Dam in Sheffield, Alabama. It would then—with the aid of floodlights—examine the dam's construction. If it could spot the flaws, it would then replace the "hard-hat" diver.

This test was observed by men from many fields. If it succeeded here, it would be used by scientists and businessmen, treasure hunters and salvage workers, cameramen and explorers. The camera itself was an inexpensive model manufactured by the Bludworth Marine Division of the Kearfott Company and costing less than four thousand dollars.

The day of the test was stormy. Rain splattered against the surface of the reservoir and the wind whipped sheets of water against the cement dam.

We sat with other witnesses in the relative comfort of a TVA barge as the camera was lowered to the bottom of the man-made lake. When all was ready, the television receiver—linked to the camera by cable—was turned on. As the image focused on the screen, we could feel the tension grow in the small cabin. The engineers and officials edged closer to the uncertain flickerings. Then the air of expectancy was suddenly replaced by excitement.

The picture was clear. Cracks and fissures, magnified three times their normal size, could easily be seen and charted.

Every man in the room enjoyed a front-row seat on the end of one era and the beginning of another. It signaled the decline of the old-fashioned helmet diving and heralded the birth of practical underwater television.

8. Skin Divers in Industry

THE SLEEK NEW JET FIGHTER PLANE sliced neatly through the mist that blanketed the California countryside. Shaking free of its cloud burden, the supersonic F4D Skyray leveled off at an altitude of four miles and hurtled west toward the Pacific Ocean.

As the streamlined craft rapidly outdistanced the sound of its own engines, the veteran test pilot decided to run it through its paces. Screaming dives, vertical ascents, full loops—the intricate gymnastics of an aerial thoroughbred on its final test flight.

Ten miles off the Malibu beaches, the airplane suddenly turned temperamental. It lost power and altitude. It failed to respond to the controls. It fell toward the ocean, drifting first like a falling leaf, then plummeting like a stone.

The test pilot frantically tried every emergency measure in the book. But it was no use. His headset crackled as instructions were relayed to him from the home base.

"Get out!" the voice said. "Jump for it before it's too late!"

The pilot needed no further encouragement. In the private language of the airman, it was "final prayer time." As he reached forward to press his ejector button, he briefly assessed his chances.

They were not good. He faced a rough and alarming fall through thin air. And then what? The chances for rescue seemed slim. The ocean, vast and empty, seemed rushing up to meet him, eager to claim him.

When the altimeter registered three thousand feet, he jabbed at the escape lever. The heart of the cockpit was disengaged, then catapulted away from the airplane. The parachute snapped open mechanically— slowing the pilot's rapid descent, jerking him into unconsciousness, supporting him like a lifeless marionette.

Even as the pilot fell, his rescuers were on the way.

The radioman back at the Douglas Aircraft Company in Santa Monica had sounded the emergency alarm. A helicopter, warmed up and standing on its short runway, fluttered up into the sky and scurried out over the ocean. The copter navigator received the exact position of the stricken aircraft over his earphones and relayed the information to the pilot.

Two fully outfitted SCUBA divers sat tensely in the cockpit of the whirlybird. This was the acid test of the world's first Heli-Diver Squadron, an integral part of the Douglas air-and-sea rescue program.

As the helicopter neared the site of the downed jet, a parachute could be seen floating on the surface of the water. The pilot, unable to free himself from the chute harness, appeared to be in a state of shock. He was only partially afloat and seemed to be sinking. There was not a moment to lose.

As the copter hovered just feet above the water's surface, skin diver Danny Dannison opened the hatch and climbed down a rope ladder. The water, churned up beneath the overhead rotor's powerful downwash, was not inviting, but Danny Dannison did not hesitate.

He dove into the water feet-first and swam underwater to the drowning man. Quickly unsnapping the parachute straps, Danny managed to tow the pilot to the surface. As he held his head above the water, Danny made a rapid on-the-spot diagnosis of the injured man's condition.

The pilot, now in a state of semiconsciousness, seemed nearer death than life. He was obviously in great pain. His right arm had been broken in two places, his left shoulder dislocated. His entire body had been bruised by the descent and subsequent impact. He also suffered from internal injuries, shock, and concussion.

Realizing that the accident victim could stand no further rough treatment, Danny Dannison decided not to risk the hazardous trip in a helicopter sling. He signaled the copter pilot that he would remain in the water until a rescue ship could arrive on the scene.

Fortunately Danny did not have long to wait. Within a few minutes a nearby lifeguard boat streaked to the scene and relieved him of his burden.

Thanks to one skin diver's courage, thanks to one industry's foresight, a man's life was saved. And just as the Heli-Divers are being used to save the lives of men, the aircraft industry is now using other skin

"PARASCUBA" is a combination of skin diving and sky diving. Note the cumbersome equipment the skin diver carries. Beside his air and other gear he is loaded with parachute and crash helmet. (photo credit on parachute photo only: *U.S. Navy Photo*)

divers to save the lives of planes.

Major plane manufacturers turned to SCUBA divers several years ago when two giant commercial airliners suddenly and mysteriously disintegrated in mid-air. The planes, both British DeHavilland Comets, were demolished during routine flights.

The entire industry was alarmed by these unexplained crashes. Scientists and engineers investigating the accidents concluded that the machines had been struck down by a strange new type of "airplane fatigue." It was found that the increased cabin pressurization required for high-altitude flights caused great stress to shudder through the airship's metal frame. This stress, occurring in cycles, had a cumulative effect—causing fatigue damage that was able to rip the entire craft apart at the seams.

These findings showed the major plane manufacturers that they would have to test future plane fuselages under greatly increased pressure loads. This had been done in the past by pumping compressed air into the passenger compartment of a newly manufactured plane. If the structure was strong enough to withstand the air pressure, it would also be able to withstand that same pressure at high altitude.

In time this proved to be a dangerous procedure. Some of the airplane fuselages exploded during the tests, frequently injuring the testing personnel.

It was then that the manufacturers added the skin diver to their staffs.

Aircraft engineers suggested that water pressure could be used in place of the dangerous air pressure. To test this theory, the Lockheed Aircraft Corporation constructed an enormous metal water tank—twenty feet wide, twenty feet deep, and one hundred feet long.

Into this empty tank they placed the fuselage of a C-130 Hercules. They then flooded the tank and the interior of the plane with water. And last of all they added two aqualung divers. The two divers descended into the huge tank and studied the airplane as it was subjected to all the stress and strain of a high-altitude flight.

We observed one of these hydrostatic tests during a recent visit to the Boeing Airplane Company in Seattle, Washington. There, in a metal pool one hundred and thirty feet long, we saw the wingless body of a new KC-135 jet airliner. Immersed in water over a year, the fuselage had been dubbed the *Stratosub*. And during that year it had undergone all the strain of many trips around the world. Before the testing would be complete, the *Stratosub* would log seventy million miles of simulated flight.

Joe Dollinger, a skin diver who often worked with local police departments in underwater searches, headed a staff of eight other expert divers assigned to the project. Before taking us down into the tank with him, Joe gave us a brief rundown of the testing procedure.

"The tank holds 420,000 gallons of water," Joe said. "The plane is pushed on all sides by a series of hydraulic jacks, generally for periods of about five minutes at a time."

"Why do you use the hydraulic jacks?"

"They duplicate all the normal flight loads on the plane," he said. "They match the strain of take-off, cabin pressurization, wind gusts, the weight of passen-

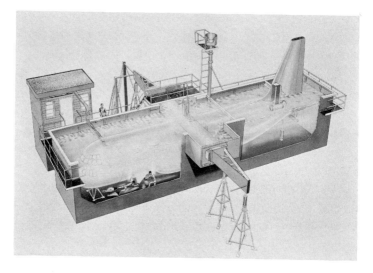

The STRATOSUB, submerged fuselage of a jet airliner, being examined by skin divers as it undergoes hydrostatic tests.

gers and cargo, and the stress of landing. In four minutes the plane undergoes all the punishment it would suffer during a complete six-hour flight."

We asked Joe why the tests had to be run under water.

"The water is pumped into and out of the airplane at a predetermined rate," he said. "The water pressure can be accurately measured, enabling us to duplicate the exact pressures of a normal flight."

After completion of the five-minute test, we followed Joe and his skin-diving comrades into the water. As engineers on the surface consulted three hundred and fifty gauges used to measure the inflicted punishment, we searched the sunken fuselage for other signs of wear and tear. The divers methodically opened and closed every door in the plane and then examined the metal seams and ribs. After finally testing the lines leading to the hydraulic jacks, we swam up from the tanks and waited for the next test.

The airplane industry is just one of many that have recently added the skin diver to the company payroll.

A team of SCUBA laborers has worked for several years in Tel Aviv, Israel, laying an enormous steel pipeline beneath the water. Chemists have used skin divers to help in the harvest of kelp for the manufacture of potash and iodine. The petroleum industry employs

Test engineers and industrial skin-diver observe pressurized water boiling up from the STRATOSUB.

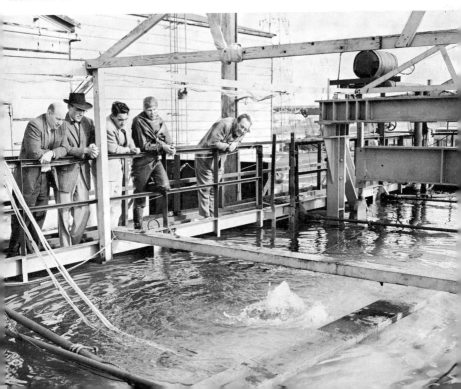

skin-diving geologists to prospect for oil along our nation's continental shelf.

The skin diver's importance to industry is now an established fact. As a result, many divers—intent on combining business with pleasure—have banded together to form their own small corporations. These Jacks-of-all-underwater-trades have found a great demand for their services, especially in the complex field of marine construction and salvage.

A young Frenchman named André Galerne opened the first skin-diving business corporation less than a decade ago. When he started out, André had two aqualungs, fifty dollars, and a do-or-die spirit.

His motto reflected his enthusiasm: "*We will do anything—anywhere—underwater.*"

The intervening years have shown that André Galerne is every bit as good as his word. His work has carried him into oceans and rivers, into dismal underwater caves and underground sewerage systems. He has helped construct a dock in Madagascar and a bridge over the Congo River.

And in the process he has accumulated a full-time staff of nearly one hundred expert skin divers. Every new applicant must face a series of difficult underwater tests before being hired. One of these tests involves the building of a wooden crate at the bottom of a swiftly flowing river. Since nails sink and boards have a tendency to float, this task requires a rare combination of ability and patience.

André Galerne's thoroughness has paid huge dividends. His organization, *SOGÉTRAM (Société Générale de Travaux Maritimes et Fluviaux)*, now has branch offices in Canada, Germany, Belgium, Switzerland, and France. Moreover, the firm's annual income is rapidly nearing the million-dollar mark.

This aqualung-to-riches success story has sparked a wave of interest in other business-minded skin divers throughout the world. To get a clear picture of their mode of operation, we visited one of the newest of these corporations last summer.

The sign over the door, freshly painted, carried a rather imposing title:

THE WILLIAMSON BROTHERS
SUB-SURFACE SALVAGE AND
REPAIR CORPORATION OF
LONG ISLAND.
John and Brad, *Proprietors*

The office itself consisted of a single, unfurnished room located near Centerton's town dock. Upon entering the office, we met the proprietors as well as the corporation's entire staff. John and Brad Williamson, two enterprising teen-agers, had been skin diving approximately half their lives.

"How's business?" we asked.

"Great," John enthused.

"Great," Brad echoed his older brother's sentiments. "In fact, we just got our first job."

As the two boys outlined the details of their first job, we found it difficult to share in their enthusiasm. To our eyes, the task seemed unappealing and perhaps impossible. An old cabin cruiser, a victim of the previous fall's hurricane, had been splintered against the rocks and now lay at the bottom of Long Island Sound. The owner had no intention of salvaging the battered craft. However, there was over a thousand dollars' worth of jewelry locked in its safe. If the Williamsons could find the launch and bring the safe to the surface, the owner offered to split the proceeds on a fifty-fifty basis.

Other, more professional salvage operations had turned down this same proposition. The Williamsons, however, welcomed the assignment. It took them nearly a week to locate the sunken cruiser. It rested beneath twenty feet of water off Eaton's Neck, a peninsula jutting out past Huntington Harbor into the waters of Long Island Sound.

The next step was to raise the safe.

"How will you do that?" we asked. "You'll need expensive equipment—a crane, a winch."

"No we won't," John replied.

"No, we won't," Brad repeated.

We could not resist the temptation of accompanying the two boys and seeking how they planned to accomplish this minor miracle. That afternoon—a blistering afternoon in August—we drove the two brothers out onto Eaton's Neck in a rented pickup truck. In the truck's storage space the two boys had deposited their aqualungs, several extra cylinders of compressed air, a length of rusting chain, and an empty oil drum.

This strange assortment of equipment answered none of our questions. We still could not understand how the boys hoped to lift the safe to the surface. Brad and John, apparently enjoying our bewilderment, volunteered no further information.

After parking the truck beside the public beach, we

helped the boys carry their equipment down to the water's edge. The tide was out and the water was lukewarm. As we waded out from the shore, the task seemed increasingly impossible. Long Island Sound has an underwater visibility of about six feet on its better days—and this was not one of its better days.

Clouds of mud had been churned up by a strong subsurface current. Clumps of seaweed floated above the murky water. And by the time the water reached our waists, we could no longer see our flippers.

The Williamson brothers carried the heavy metal chain, the rusted oil drum, and an extra cylinder of compressed air with them. Before submerging, they attached the length of chain to the drum. The empty container floated on the surface and supported the weight of the chain.

John towed the floating oil drum to a spot about fifty yards off the shore. Brad carried the cylinder of air and we followed at his heels. At a depth of about ten feet the nature of the water suddenly changed. It became much colder but it was also relatively clear. Although the surface congestion blocked out most of the sun's rays, we were able to distinguish the remains of the sunken vessel.

The launch had undergone terrible punishment during its pounding against the rocks, and the sea had robbed it of any remaining dignity. Mud inched up against its broken hull. Seaweed entombed it in a veil of green. The metal was rusting and the wood was rotting. Barnacles clung to the anchor chain. Black water marked the site of gaping wounds leading to the heart of the craft.

This actually was the first encouraging sign. The disintegration of the ship eliminated the need for acetylene torches. The storm had performed an operation that bettered any man-made surgery.

Our momentary optimism was quickly dispelled when we first saw the safe. The square metal container sat in an exposed portion of the cabin. Old-fashioned and bulky, the strongbox probably weighed in the neighborhood of five hundred pounds.

As we studied the object, Brad swam down from the surface with the metal oil drum. He had partially filled it with water so that it would submerge. John reached for the end of the attached chain and wrapped it securely around the strongbox.

Only then did we begin to understand their plan. Only then did we begin to appreciate their ingenuity.

After securing the chain to the safe, the boys then turned their attention to the spare tank of compressed air. They affixed the cylinder nozzle to the valve at the base of the submerged oil drum. They then proceeded to pump the compressed air into it. As the air entered the drum, the water was slowly forced out. And after a very few moments the drum began to rise in the water, and soon hovered directly above the safe.

It was difficult to believe that such a simple and inexpensive device could lift the safe. However, the boys later explained that they had learned in basic physics that one cubic foot of air would support a weight of sixty-two pounds in water.

As still more air was forced into the metal drum, the chain stretched taut. The old safe turned over on its side then slowly, reluctantly, began its ascent. Moments later the improvised buoy floated on the surface. The safe was suspended just four feet beneath it.

As we returned to the pickup truck, Brad and John remained in the water and towed the floating prize in toward the town dock. The hoist normally used to lift boats from the water then hoisted the safe onto the rear of the pickup truck. We drove the two SCUBA businessmen directly to the owner's home and watched him rub his eyes in disbelief when he recognized the safe.

"Congratulations, boys," he said later, writing out a check for five hundred dollars. "I didn't think it was possible."

Brad solemnly filled out an official receipt for the money and John examined the check.

"Five hundred dollars!" John exclaimed. "That's pretty good pay for one day's work."

We could not help but agree with the enterprising young man. However, as many skin-diving businessmen have discovered, each job is a gamble. And often their only reward is the pleasure of diving. The Williamson brothers learned this lesson the following morning.

On arriving at their office, we noticed several decorative additions. A brand-new telephone, installed that morning, sat proudly on a scarred secondhand office desk. The old safe that they had retrieved the previous day had been scrubbed down, repainted, and left to dry in a corner of the room.

The boys had evidently invested the remainder of their first fee during an early morning tour of the local boat yards, metal shops, and junk yards. The newly purchased equipment consisted of a war-surplus magnetic metals detector, an oxy-arc torch, and a small pneumatic hammer—all apparently in need of major overhauls. A small sign propped on the desk carried the corporation's brand-new motto: *"No job too big, no job too small."*

As we were expressing proper admiration over the additions, the telephone rang. Brad pounced on the receiver before it could emit a second ring and answered it in his most businesslike voice. Recognizing his sister's voice, he listened for several moments, then replaced the phone in its cradle. It was then that we saw an example of the enthusiasm that is so necessary to any skin diver planning on entering business for himself.

"Is it another job?" John asked.

"Well—yes and no," Brad replied. "It was Sis. She got mad at her boy friend last night and tossed her engagement ring off the Centerton Bridge. Now she's changed her mind. She wants the guy back; only first she has to get the ring back. She doesn't have any money."

"Are we going to do it?"

"Sure we are," Brad philosophized. "Who are we to stand in the way of true love? Besides, *'No job too big, no job too small'*—that's our motto, isn't it?"

9. The Last Frontier

HISTORY is the story of man in conquest.

It is the story of pioneers, of explorers who dared cross new frontiers to chart paths through the wilderness. A courageous Italian sea captain who sailed the Atlantic and discovered a new world; two American brothers who constructed a box-shaped machine able to lift them into the air in defiance of gravity's invisible bonds; a bearded Frenchman who explored the narrow confines of a test tube and discovered a cure for rabies—these are all men in conquest.

One by one the barriers of this planet have been conquered. The oceans have been crossed. The mountains have been climbed. The jungles have been mapped.

There is just one great frontier remaining on earth. This is the world beneath the oceans and seas, the dark, unexplored wilderness now being charted by the skin diver. For centuries man has sailed and lived on the water. Today he is taking his first, hesitant steps to chart the world beneath the surface.

No one knows for sure what he will find. Beyond this last frontier exists a vast world that dwarfs our continents and makes a mockery of our mountains. Three hundred million cubic miles of ocean and sea are spread over three-quarters of the world's surface. In fact if the earth were smooth—unmarked by mountain or by valley—all land would lie buried beneath two miles of water.

The history of diving goes back many centuries, back beyond the written records of the world's first historians.

Anthropologists, uncovering a civilization that existed nearly seven thousand years ago, learned that ancient Mesopotamian divers gathered large quantities of mother-of-pearl, used for ornaments and decoration. Sixth-dynasty Thebes, dating back three thousand years before the birth of Christ, also employed divers for the same purpose. And about that same time an ancient Cretan civilization used divers to gather murex mollusks for making a purple coloring agent.

Many early civilizations built beside tropical waters are known to have gathered pearls, corals, and sponges from the sea.

The first written mention of diving appears in Homer's *Iliad*. The great Greek poet humorously compared a charioteer that had been thrown from his cart to an oyster diver:

> *Ye Gods! With what facility he dives!*
> *Ah! It were well if, in the fishy deep,*
> *The man were occupied—he might no few*
> *With oysters satisfy.*

Alexander the Great as a diver, portrayed in a 13th-century French manuscript.

The world's first historians, Thucydides and Herodotus, tell many tales of the first ancient frogmen. Xerxes, a Persian monarch five centuries before the birth of Christ, hired a Greek diver named Scyllis to recover treasure from his own sunken ships. The Athenians turned to the underwater warriors to saw down submarine barriers during the siege of Syracuse.

About this same time man began to experiment with his first underwater breathing apparatus. This problem of breathing beneath the sea was to defy many of the world's greatest thinkers. Aristotle, writing during the fourth century B.C., described the first snorkel when he told of men attempting to draw air through a tube suspended above the surface. However, the water pressure made this device practical only a few inches beneath the surface.

Fifteen centuries later the English writer and philosopher Roger Bacon was still concerned with the problem of carrying an air supply beneath the surface. Early in the sixteenth century, Leonardo da Vinci sketched plans for a diving suit that contained a cylinder of air, weighted belts, and a diving mask.

A seventeenth-century Italian mathematician, Giovanni Borelli, designed a recirculating device similar to that used by Commander Crabb and his frogmen during World War II. This invention was based on the theory that a diver's exhaled air could be purified, filtered, and returned to him in usable form. However, Signor Borelli was several centuries ahead of his time and his device proved impractical when tested.

An Englishman named Edmund Halley invented a wooden diving bell in 1716. Men standing beneath the large cup-shaped vat could breathe the trapped air. Additional air was lowered to the divers in large weighted barrels, enabling them to stay beneath the water for over an hour at a time. However, since their movements were strictly limited, this invention had little value other than as a novelty.

As the years passed, more and more inventors turned

their attention toward a device that would permit man to breathe under water. They used large metal pipes, leather tubes, goatskin air bags, lowered barrels, oversized bellows—but all to no avail. As time passed, it became clear that the air would have to be pumped down to the diver.

The development of the air compressor—a machine that could pump air below the water—enabled divers to work at a depth of fifty feet by the year 1800.

This paved the way for the invention of the world's first practical diving suit, developed by England's Augutus Siebe in 1819. Known as "open dress," this apparatus consisted basically of a helmet linked to a

A diving bell such as this was successfully used by Halley, 18th-century scientist, for periods up to an hour and a half. Fresh air was sent from the surface by alternating barrels, connected to bell by leather hoses.

metal shoulder plate that was fastened to a leather jacket. The pump forced compressed air through an inlet valve on the helmet and the exhaled air escaped beneath the diver's loose-fitting jacket. Unfortunately, however, should the diver stumble and fall, water would rush into the "open dress" and flood his helmet.

Consequently Siebe invented a "closed-dress" suit in 1837. This suit was airtight and exhaled air escaped through a second helmet valve. This principle, with very few modifications, is still used by the modern "hard-hat" divers.

During this same period, another Englishman was experimenting with the world's first SCUBA. W. H. James fastened a metal cylinder of compressed air to the diver's waist. However, since there was no way of regulating the flow of air, this great-grandaddy of the aqualung was effective for only a few moments at a time. Another self-contained breathing device, developed in 1878 by Britain's Henry Fleuss, used the oxygen rebreathing principle established earlier by Borelli. The carbon dioxide in the exhaled air was trapped in a solution of caustic potash, and the purified oxygen was returned to the diver for new use. Since pure oxygen proved poisonous to deep sea divers—crippling the central nervous system and causing severe convulsions and frequent fatalities—almost all underwater work was done by the helmeted diver until a very few years ago.

Today's skin diver takes his freedom of movement for granted. He would find it difficult to imagine the tremendous difference between SCUBA diving and old-fashioned helmet diving. During our reporting for an earlier book we had one opportunity to dive in hard-hat dress. It was an experience that we can still vividly recall.

That first dive took place in shallow water off the coast of Florida that borders the Gulf of Mexico. Most shallow-water work was then done in relatively simple equipment, often just a helmet and a metal shoulder support. However, we were anxious to experience the sensations of the deep-sea diver and asked for the full treatment.

Before even seeing our diving helmets, we had to step into the traditional heavy woolen underwear and socks. Then—with the assistance of two other divers—we literally climbed into a diving suit made of extra-thick vulcanized rubber. The suit was open at the neck and wrists. Unwieldy three-finger gloves were hooked over the watertight wrist cuffs. The legs of our diving dress were laced tightly so that no air could enter.

A heavy metal breastplate, the base for the helmet, was then fastened to our suit's shoulders and chest. Our diving shoes turned out to be enormous wood and brass structures that were clearly designed in the interest of utility, not fashion. Lead weights used to cancel under-water instability added fifteen pounds to the weight of each shoe. The shoes were both laced and buckled to make sure that neither air nor water could enter.

As we tottered on these weighted pedestals, our diving belts were carried to us. Each leather belt was six inches in width and carried an additional hundred pounds of lead. These, too, had to be tightly laced.

We were melting in the great heat of the outfits, as though we were lifting weights in an oven. However, we were not yet ready to dive. As we sat down, our assistants carried the heavy metal diving helmets to us.

These were slipped over our heads and bolted securely to the metal breastplates. We found our heads closed into a tiny space. Each viewing window was less than four inches in diameter.

Speaking through a radio set, our instructors told us how to use the two breathing valves on the side of the helmet—the exhaust and intake valves. One knob adjusted the flow of air into the helmet. A lever, set just beneath our chins, regulated the flow of exhaled air. After the viewing windows were closed and bolted, the compressor began to pump a hissing stream of air into our helmets.

Our earphones crackled with a most welcome bit of information: it was finally time to begin our first helmeted dive. Standing up, we discovered that ordinary movement was impossible. There was a good reason for this: with complete equipment, we each tipped the scales at about four hundred pounds.

The two experienced divers helped us totter over to the Jacob's ladder leading from the side of the boat to the water. Perspiration drenched us and the helmet pushed down against our shoulders. Each step down the ladder required a major effort. As we stepped into the water, the increased pressure wrapped our rubber trousers tightly around our legs. The immediate cooling effect of the water was highly gratifying.

However, even with the decrease in our weight we enjoyed less freedom than marionettes on strings. One man operated the winch that controlled all of our vertical movements. A second operator manned the air compressor, supplying us with our life-giving air.

Diving with an aqualung.

Once we reached the bay floor, we discovered that walking was a process that had to be learned all over again. We walked stiffly, like knights encased in inflexible armor. Simple acts such as picking up a pebble became as difficult as picking up a dime while wearing leather mittens.

We were no longer in control of ourselves. We were mechanical robots who depended on machinery for our very lives. Today it would be an easy matter to duplicate that dive with the freedom of an aqualung. But at that time the aqualung was merely a toy being used by a group of adventurous Frenchmen.

The aqualung—the invention that permits the modern skin diver to enjoy the mobility and comfort of a fish—

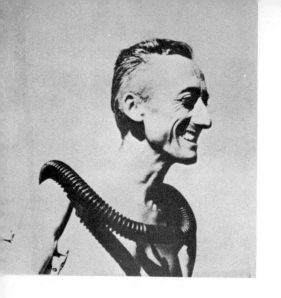

"Father of the Aqualung" Captain Jacques Cousteau is co-inventor of SCUBA.

is the result of the dedication and ingenuity of a small group of French naval officers.

As far back as 1925 Commander Le Prieur began experimenting with a cylinder of compressed air. Unlike pressurized oxygen, this invention permitted the diver to go deeper than thirty-five feet without suffering any toxic effects. However, there was still no way of regulating the wasteful flow of air. Ten years later Commander Louis de Corlieu invented the first practical swim fins. The face mask, a lineal descendant of diving goggles used by native fishermen, had been developed in 1865 by Benoit Rouquayrol and August Denayrouze.

In 1936 a twenty-five-year-old Frenchman named Jacques-Yves Cousteau tried on his first pair of underwater goggles. Many years later he was to recall that experience in his splendid book, *The Silent World*.

"Sometimes we are lucky enough to know that our lives have been changed, to discard the old, embrace the new and run headlong down an immutable course. It happened to me at Le Mourillon on that summer's day, when my eyes were opened on the sea."

Jacques-Yves Cousteau has passionately embraced the world of the sea during most of his life. Even as a boy he expressed an interest in becoming a sailor. After graduating from the Brest Naval Academy, he rapidly worked his way up the ranks of the French Navy. He received certificates qualifying him as a navigator, a gunner, an aerial observer, and a master. Today he is fully qualified to command any ship in the French fleet. His heroism with the French underground movement during World War II merited him both the Legion of Honor and the *Croix de guerre.*

However, history will remember Captain Cousteau not for his naval accomplishments on the surface, but rather for his pioneering excursions beneath the sea. It began that day in 1936 when his eyes were first "opened on the sea."

Since then Captain Cousteau has searched for downed airplanes, for sunken treasure, for archaeological discoveries. His underwater camera work produced films that won the Grand Prize at Venice, Cannes, Paris and an Academy Award in the United States. The founder of the famed Group for Underwater Research, he is now Director of the French Underwater Center as well as the Oceanographic Museum of Monaco. In addition he is the President of the World Underwater Confederation, a group of sports divers from thirty-two nations.

Captain Cousteau has made nearly two thousand

dives into the sea. However, one dive stays in his memory above all others. This particular underwater excursion took place in June of 1943. The only witnesses were local fishermen and close friends who watched him walk down a sandy beach of the French Riviera.

This was the first dive ever made with an aqualung.

For a period of many months, Captain Cousteau had been secretly working with his friend Emile Gagnan. The two men designed and invented a compressed-air breathing device that would supply air to the diver only when he needed it. This was accomplished by an air regulator, a valve to stop the wasteful flow of air except when the diver inhaled.

The lobster fishermen who saw Captain Cousteau that day shrugged their shoulders and laughed. He looked like a man from outer space. A strange, glass-windowed mask covered his eyes and nose. Fishlike rubber fins shielded his feet. Seven pounds of lead weight were fastened to his belt. And, most laughable of all, three cylinders of compressed air were mounted on his back.

This is almost precisely the same equipment used by the SCUBA diver of today. But then it was just another untested invention, a device with limitless possibilities and no known capabilities. Even Captain Cousteau was unsure. He waded cautiously into the water. He swam slowly at first, accustoming himself to breathing through an air regulator. He then decided to try a few experiments. The results of those tests were graphically recorded in *The Silent World*.

"I experimented with all possible maneuvers of the

aqualung—loops, somersaults and barrel rolls. I stood upside down on one finger and burst out laughing, a shrill distorted laugh. Nothing I did altered the automatic rhythm of air. Delivered from gravity and buoyancy I flew around in space."

Since that pioneering swim countless other divers have shared Captain Cousteau's exuberance over the complete freedom of "flying around in space." However, this last frontier would not have been opened were it not for one man's combination of courage and creativity—a man who has been rightly called the "father of the aqualung" and the "submarine Buck Rogers"— Captain Jacques-Yves Cousteau.

The aqualung, ideal for free movement in depths not exceeding three hundred feet, has proven dangerous for work that must be done in deeper water. Some industrial and salvage projects must still be carried out by hard-hat divers. Working in the tremendous pressure that exists five hundred feet beneath the surface, most commercial divers wear a heavy, inflexible suit known technically as "articulated rigid dress." The diver in this suit—able to bend his elbows only with the assistance of a ball-and-socket mechanism—has about as much mobility as a sardine jammed into a tin can.

And even this armor becomes useless below a depth of seven hundred feet. While this might seem like a considerable distance to the skin diver, it is actually barely scratching the ocean's potential. The ocean floors are not flat; they are broken by enormous mountain ranges and ravines that sometimes plummet seven miles into the heart of the earth.

Scientists have always speculated about the possibility

of life existing in these valleys, in this vast world of "inner space." It was clear that only a superstrong underwater vehicle could ever probe the depths. Alexander the Great is reported to have retached the bottom of a river in a crude wooden diving bell. And the remarkable English author H. G. Wells drew up amazingly accurate plans for the modern diving bell in his short story. "In the Abyss."

However, it was up to one man to turn the early theories and legends into modern scientific reality. That man is the famous Swiss scientist, Auguste Piccard. For more than a quarter of a century Dr. Piccard has channeled all of his energy and ingenuity into the development of a deep-water diving vehicle.

After several false starts he invented the diving bell known as a bathyscaphe. Two men were able to sit in this circular container constructed of thick steel with lucite viewing windows. This metal bubble, more than six feet in diameter, received its power from an electric motor that drove twin propellers.

The bathyscaphe was suspended beneath a balloon-like container holding ten thousand gallons of gasoline. The gas was not used as fuel, but as a type of underwater parachute. Lighter than water, the petroleum could be used for buoyancy when rising from the ocean floor.

Dr. Piccard's most modern bathyscaphe, the *Trieste*, was recently shipped to the island of Guam. With the inventor's son Jacques at the controls, the *Trieste* was lowered into a gully known as the Challenger Deep. This is the deepest known spot in the underwater world. Jacques Piccard, pilot of the bathyscaphe on sixty-four previous voyages, was joined by an American, Dr.

Robert Dietz of the Navy Electronics Laboratory.

The two men guided the *Trieste* to the almost incredible depth of 35,800 feet, establishing a depth record that is unlikely to be broken. In the process they demonstrated that earth's last frontier—its oceans and seas—can now be explored.

10. Matadors of the Sea

WHY does he do it?

Why does the skin diver—frail, fragile, vulnerable— enter the mysterious and sometimes hostile world beneath the sea?

This is an ancient riddle. Why does the bullfighter— armed with a small red cape draped over a slender sword—stand up before two tons of onrushing muscle and horn? Why does the mountain climber inch his way across a vertical sheet of ice set halfway between a precipice and sudden death?

The matador explains that the bull is not his enemy; they are partners involved in a graceful and deadly search. Together they unearth the courage and fear buried deep in the soul of man. The mountain climber is not merely ascending a peak on the earth's landscape. He is conquering something within himself. The mountain serves his purpose because, as George Mallory once said, "it is there."

Compared to these endeavors, skin diving may seem

as safe as a guided tour through a museum of natural history. And so it is—with most divers. Man enters the water in search of knowledge, beauty, gold, or perhaps just a leisurely stroll through a strange new garden.

However, there are some skin divers who actively seek out the challenges of the sea. They photograph sharks and lasso porpoises. They carve holes in the ice and plunge into subfreezing water. They dive the deepest, stay the longest, swim the farthest. The sea is their partner and danger is their ever-faithful companion. Seeking out the very limits of the underwater world, they discover the limits of man.   .

These are the matadors of the sea. These are the skin divers in competition—in competition with each other, in competition with themselves.

Such a man is Jeremiah Haskell, a broad-shouldered professional wildcat hunter in the state of Washington. Jerry's business carries him into forest and mountain as he tracks the wily cougars, the giant cats who feed on defenseless deer.

Between hunts Jerry rests up in his cottage in Lilliwaup, a small hamlet set in the shadows of the Olympic Mountains on the rocky shore of Puget Sound. When we met Jerry, he was taking a busman's holiday—preparing to embark on another kind of hunt, one that makes cougar-tracking seem tame in comparison.

"I think I'll go get me an octopus," he told us one pleasant morning in early September.

"Octopus?" Our question reflected our skepticism. "Fine. Suppose you manage actually to get an octopus —what would you do with him then?"

"Why, then maybe we'd just wrestle a bit," he said.

"Come on along—it's a fine sport. Those little fellows can put up a stiff fight."

Although we had never seen an octopus outside of an aquarium, we didn't take Jerry seriously for a single moment. We did not then believe that any man would consider grappling with the repugnant, many-armed devilfish. Victor Hugo, the famous French author, described a terrifying and bloody battle with an octopus in his book *Toilers of the Sea*. Since then countless Hollywood movies have added to the legend by habitually picturing the octopus as a brutal man-killer.

While we realized these tales might be somewhat exaggerated, we also knew that there were many authenticated accounts of octopuses attacking and drowning native pearl divers in the South Pacific. We assumed that Jerry was playing a prank on his old friends. Laughingly agreeing to help him hunt the devilfish, we asked him what kind of spear gun he planned to use.

"Spear gun?" He seemed surprised. "Now, that wouldn't be sporting, would it? Using a spear gun with an aqualung—the very idea!"

"You mean you use your bare hands?"

"Some prefer to wear gloves," he replied. "And don't forget to bring your diving suits. That water gets mighty cold down at the bottom."

The following morning we carried our aqualungs to Jerry's boat, a compact eighteen-foot power launch that he had built in his garage. Still unconvinced, we expected him to admit that it was all a prank. However, he made no such admission. Instead Jerry proceeded to amaze us with his intimate knowledge of the octopus during our two-hour trip to the hunting site.

"There are many types of octopus," he said. "Over one hundred and fifty known varieties. Fortunately the Puget Sound octopus is one of the bigger ones—big enough to put up an interesting fight."

"*Fortunately?* Just how big does the Puget Sound octopus grow?"

"The largest one we've ever wrestled here spanned about fourteen feet," he replied. "They claim they've caught them up in Alaska at better than thirty feet. We'll be lucky to catch us a ten-footer."

"That's lucky?"

"There's nothing to be afraid of," he said. "They've never hurt me yet, and I've been doing this for about three years."

"How about those tentacles?" we asked. "They're supposed to be strong enough to squeeze a man to death."

"In the first place, an octopus has arms, not tentacles," he corrected our terminology. "The decopoda, his relative, has tentacles—ten of them. The octopus has only eight arms."

"Well, how about the arms then? Aren't they supposed to be fairly powerful?"

"Don't get me wrong; they're plenty powerful," he said. "Each one of those arms has a double row of suction discs, and those little suckers are used as an anchor. The octopus wraps two or three of his arms around a rock while the rest are out feeling around for his supper."

"What do they eat for supper?"

"Not skin divers, generally speaking," he tried to reassure us. "They seem to prefer crabs or small bottom

Skin-diving octopus wrestler brings ashore his defeated adversary—a 56 pound monster. (*Wide World Photos*)

fish. Then, too, they've been known to crawl up on shore. Natives in the South Pacific claim they catch mice and rabbits. But I've never heard of their eating a man."

"Do they have sharp teeth?"

"They're called radula, not teeth," he said. "But supposedly they have another weapon—a kind of hypodermic needle they use to inject a nerve poison into their victims. I've never met anyone who was bitten, but there are some cases on record."

As our surface journey ended, we began to sense that Jeremiah Haskell might be quite serious about the entire unbelievable business. We moored the boat in a protected bay and walked out to the tip of an adjacent point. As we tested our breathing apparatus, we glanced out at the water. It looked dark and foreboding. The land seemed to fall rapidly from the shore line.

"This is the spot," Jerry announced. "Just let me give you a few pointers. If you should become entangled with an octopus, don't hesitate to use your knife. Jab it between the eyes. You'll hit the brain center and the animal should die immediately."

Anticipating our next questions, Jerry then outlined the unofficial rules and regulations for the sport of octopus-wrestling. After luring the octopus from his hole, we were to grab him before he could grab us. And then, according to Jerry, it would be a simple matter to drag him back to shore.

"Just one question—how do we lure them from their caves?"

"Well, if we were in the Hawaiian Islands we would probably use the bait preferred by the local octopus hunters. They use another skin diver for bait. Once the octopus wraps his arms around the poor fellow, the second diver swims down and bites as hard as he can into the animal's brain."

"With his *teeth?*"

"Don't worry," he said, smiling. "We're not in the Hawaiian Islands. On Puget Sound we seldom use another skin diver as bait. As a matter of fact, our bait is a closely guarded secret. If people found out what we used, they'd flock here. Everyone and his maiden aunt would go octopus-hunting and there wouldn't be any left for us old-timers."

Although we seriously doubted whether anyone's "maiden aunt" would rush to stalk the devilfish, we nonetheless vowed not to divulge the secret of the bait.

As we waded out into the sound, we could see that the water was alive with fish. The fall salmon run had started and great silver Kings and Chinooks leaped high into the air. The misshapen backs of the Humpies and Doggies broke water as the salmon swept by us on their annual trip back to the rivers of their birth.

Submerging and following Jerry, we saw that the shore line was actually a cliff that fell many fathoms into an underwater ravine. At a depth of approximately sixty feet the earth leveled out into a plateau that was broken by boulders and scattered rock formations. The flat flounders and sole rested on the muddy bottom. The shadowy forms of ling cod and rock cod flitted through the dimly lighted water surrounding the rocks.

Less than one minute after reaching the bottom we sighted our first octopus. Jerry, staring into the ebony mouth of a small cave at the base of three boulders, motioned us back with a wave of his hand. Two thin, snakelike structures projected from the black opening. These, we soon learned, were the tips of two arms.

Backing cautiously away from the cave, Jerry remained out of the beast's line of sight. He placed his secret bait just barely within the octopus's reach and waited, as the tip of one arm flicked tentatively against the lure. Then the second arm reached out, followed in short order by a third and a fourth.

The arms, slender at the ends, were heavy and muscular in the center. As they uncoiled and stretched out, we could see that they were about four feet in length. Their color changed from black to gray as they emerged from the cave. A double row of white suction cups lined the underside of the squirming, writhing arms.

The eight arms met at the animal's "neck," the narrow base of its small globular body. The head was built like a light bulb covered with ugly little bumps. It was easily the most sinister animal we have ever encountered under water, and we understood immediately why many fishermen refer to it as the devilfish.

After the octopus had uncoiled all of its arms, Jerry dropped the bait. As the animal's arms enveloped the lure, Jerry made his move. Literally leaping into the center of the squirming mass, he clutched the animal's body.

Bracing himself against one of the rocks, he jerked the octopus away from the ground. However, one of the animal's eight arms had remained securely anchored around a boulder. It was then that we saw the tremendous power of the suction discs. Instead of releasing its grip, the arm was literally ripped from its socket as Jerry started lifting it toward the surface. This, we later learned, is not uncommon among octopuses.

Remaining a cautious distance behind the trailing arms, we followed Jerry as he forced his catch back to shore. As we joined him on the beach, he was critically appraising his recent acquisition.

"Shucks, it's just a baby," he commented. "Hardly

big enough to make a good chowder. But don't worry. We'll find his daddy during our next trip down. And then it'll be your turn."

Luckily Jerry's optimism proved to be unjustified. Although we did manage to locate some of his little brothers, we never did find an octopus large enough to qualify as his father.

Later that afternoon Jerry tenderized our catch by thoroughly mashing the octopus meat with the flat side of a single-bitted ax. Then, after boiling the edible portions, he added carrots, potatoes, celery stalks, onions, and seasoning to the broth. Although we knew that candied octopus is considered a rare delicacy in Spain, we approached our devilfish supper with some misgivings. However, we were most pleasantly surprised. Firm and white, the octopus meat was comparable in flavor to that of the Maine lobster.

Then and there we made a mental resolution. We resolved to limit our future octopus-hunting to steaming chowders, and to avoid looking for the animal in dark caves.

Other, more adventurous souls, however, seem to thrive on the sport of octopus-wrestling. It all began five years ago when Jack Meyers, a member of the Puget Sound Mudsharks, engaged his first octopus in hand-to-hand combat. His success caused his skin-diving comrades to dub him "Mighty Meyers, the Octopus-Killer." Since then the sport has grown in popularity. Recently a team of octopus wrestlers from the United States competed with Canada in the first international octopus hunt.

Competition between aqualung enthusiasts covers

every aspect of skin diving. Annual spearfishing contests, sanctioned by the Amateur Athletic Union, attract both male and female skin divers. Many skin-diving clubs regularly test their members with organized treasure hunts, starfish-gathering contests, and underwater photography competitions.

However, this all seems like child's play in comparison to the most treacherous underwater sport of them all. For, the greatest peril exists not when one man competes against another. The real danger appears when the skin diver competes against the record book, against his own natural limitations.

The story of the depth divers—the courageous, sometimes foolhardy swimmers who long to go deeper than anyone before them—began well before the birth of the aqualung.

Japanese and Polynesian pearl divers, using no artificial breathing apparatus, regularly reached depths of eighty feet in the course of their work. And Captain Cousteau has told of a sixty-year-old sponge fisherman who went down one hundred and thirty feet and remained there two and one-half minutes with no ill effects.

The most amazing dive of all reportedly took place back in 1913. Although this occurred before the keeping of records, reputable eyewitnesses claim that a young Greek named Stotti Georghies descended 200 feet to recover a lost anchor.

These incredible depths could never be reached by an ordinary swimmer using ordinary techniques. These divers spent a great deal of their lives beneath the surface of the water. They had to be in splendid physical and mental condition for the tortuous descent beneath the one-hundred-foot level.

In addition, most of the free-dive depth records were set by men who were masters of hyperventilation—a breathing technique that enabled them to stay under water far longer than the normal man. Before diving, the swimmer would take an extended series of short, explosive breaths. Then, at precisely the right moment, he would change the tempo and begin breathing in enormous, lung-filling breaths of air. Holding the last deep inhalation, he then plunged to the depths.

Following the invention of the aqualung, the skin diver was able to reach new depths—and new dangers.

The great pressure of deep water affects man's body in many ways. The record-seeking skin diver found that he had to follow the decompression tables used by helmet divers to avoid a crippling or fatal attack of the bends. This entailed a slow ascent interrupted periodically by resting spells—pauses that would permit compressed nitrogen to escape from the body.

During the early days of the aqualung, each dive below two hundred feet produced a new world record. Until the year 1947 no diver had gone beneath 210 feet, a mark set by Captain Cousteau's constant diving companion, Frédéric Dumas. That summer Captain Cousteau descended to the unheard-of level of 294 feet.

And the race was on.

Dumas countered that same year with a dive that carried him 306 feet beneath the surface. When their close friend Maurice Farques extended the mark to 394 feet, disaster struck. Succumbing to the pleasant but lethal affects of nitrogen narcosis, Maurice Farques was overcome by sleep and drowned.

At this point Cousteau attempted to end the race for new records. "The death of Farques and the lessons of the summer showed that three hundred feet is the extreme boundary of compressed-air diving," he wrote.

However, other skin divers did not heed the wise words of the inventor of the aqualung. The depth divers felt that the four-hundred-foot level could be reached, just as the four-minute mile could be run. Time and again they descended beyond the limits of sanity. And by the year 1957 over two hundred divers had lost their lives in futile efforts to establish new records.

That year a California skin diver named Smokey Ream made a nearly successful attempt to reach the depth of four hundred feet. This was one of the best-planned depth dives in SCUBA history. Smokey Ream, a wiry diver with many years of experience, was no novice, no amateur.

A mere glance at his dive should be enough to discourage any other would-be record setters.

Smokey Ream had invented a new type of air regulator, one that would force him to continue breathing even if he should fall asleep in deep water. Instead of using standard compressed-air cylinders, he filled his tanks with a mixture of helium and oxygen to help ward off the deadly nitrogen narcosis. Each tank cost eighty dollars, and he needed a total of twenty-five for the dive.

For protection against the cold, he wore two diving suits, constructed of heavy neoprene. His hood was a quarter of an inch in thickness. His gloves were cut from heavy leather. Further to insure his safety, he followed a chain, painted luminous yellow, beneath the three-hundred-foot depth. And to insure a rapid descent, he carried four hundred pounds of lead attached to his diving belt.

After receiving an injection of vitamins and gulping some oxygenation capsules, Smokey Ream began his descent. Going down was the easy part. And even then, because of a mechanical mix-up, he stopped his descent twenty feet shy of the four-hundred-foot marker. He attached a piece of wire to the chain, the flag that was later to prove his conquest of this great depth.

As he started to return toward the surface, he discovered that he was unable to cut loose the tremendous weight that he had worn as ballast. Consequently he had to carry four hundred pounds of superfluous lead all the way back to the surface with him.

The added effort almost cost him his life. Over a hundred feet beneath the surface he began to feel the first pains—the initial signs of the bends. By the time he reached the surface, Smokey Ream's body was twisted in agonizing pain. He was rushed to nearby Terminal Island and the large decompression chamber manned by the United States Navy.

Smokey Ream's survival was a miracle—a tribute to his extensive preparations, to his top physical condition, to the prompt medical treatment.

Two years later three Italian skin divers shattered all existing records with a dive that carried them four hundred and thirty feet beneath the waters of Naples Gulf. Ennio Falco, Alberto Novelli, and Cesar Olgiai made the dive with compressed air.

Instead of bringing an end to the race, this superhuman effort only inspired a new wave of record seekers, men who want to dive the deepest. Like the mountain climber and the bullfighter, they are searching for the courage and conquering the fears that lie deep within themselves. These are the matadors of the sea.

11. The First Dive

THE SKIN DIVER enters a strange new world of peace and tranquillity. The winds may blow and the rains may fall, but the turbulence above is not felt below. The sounds of civilization are muffled, and even the colors are muted. The gravity that anchors man to earth is forgotten. Troubles, burdens, worries—these, too, dissolve in the calm world beneath the sea.

But it can also be a jungle, a world of sudden danger and unexpected violence. Man-eating sharks swim serenely beside the razor-toothed moray eel. The jewel-toned Portuguese man-of-war lives in poisonous harmony with the warted lionfish. The killer whale—the most vicious animal of the sea—roams here with impunity.

Fortunately most skin divers will never encounter a killer whale or an attacking shark. The real dangers—inexperience, ignorance, carelessness—are with the diver when he first goes beneath the surface.

Man, a recent intruder in this underwater world, is

his own worst enemy. He has no natural equipment that will permit him to live beneath the sea. Since he cannot breathe as a fish does, he must carry a bottle of air on his back. Since his frail body cannot withstand the cold, he must wear a protective suit. He covers his eyes with a mask of glass and anchors himself with a belt of lead weights. Since his movements are slow and restricted, he straps flippers to his feet.

And still he is vulnerable. He remains a tourist, a sightseer in a foreign environment that is not always hospitable. He can afford no careless acts, no errors in judgment. His first misstep may well be his last. Consequently those first steps into the underwater world should be slow, cautious ones. Before even donning his aqualung, he should fully understand the dangers that await him. Before attempting the depths, he should master the shallows. Before trusting himself, he should swim beside an expert diver.

These lessons were brought home to us with some force before we ever contemplated skin diving.

Frank Randall, a sandy-haired fourteen-year-old boy who lives near us on Long Island, had been swimming since he first learned to walk. On his birthday his parents presented him with a shining new aqualung. This well-intentioned gift was as dangerous as presenting a child with a loaded revolver.

After glancing quickly through the instruction booklet, Frank Randall made the near-fatal error of thinking he could use the equipment without expert instruction. As a result, he entered the water understanding neither the limitations of SCUBA nor the limitations of his own body.

Luckily the youth tested his aqualung at a beach being used by a local skin-diving club. This fact alone saved his life.

After strapping on the cylinders of compressed air and trying out the mouthpiece, Frank waded confidently into the shallow bay waters of Manorhaven Beach. He discovered that it was quite a simple matter to breathe the compressed air. Then, deciding to come back up to the surface, Frank made the error of holding his breath.

Even as his head broke water, he realized that something had gone wrong. His arms and his legs felt stiff. Walking over to one of the experienced skin divers, Frank attempted to ask what had happened to him. However, his words were blurred and fuzzy.

The veteran diver, a SCUBA instructor named Dick Matt, took one look at the boy and realized what had happened. Scooping up Frank in his muscular arms, Dick Matt carried him rapidly up toward the beach. He stopped beside a contraption that looked like an oversized tin can with a door and window. Opening the door, he eased the boy into the airtight metal cylinder. He then turned on a valve that pumped compressed air into the container.

Although Frank did not know it then, this was a re-compression chamber. As the internal pressure mounted, he began to feel his symptoms disappear. Unwilling to take chances, Dick Matt had the compact unit rushed to a nearby hospital. Frank was then transferred to a room-sized recompression chamber where doctors could enter and treat him.

Frank Randall was one of the luckier ones. Without

this prompt treatment he would probably have lost his life. He had suffered from a mild attack of air embolism, the most common cause of fatalities among inexperienced skin divers.

However, if he had known more about basic physics, he could have easily avoided his brush with death.

Our bodies are constantly subjected to pressure. On dry land the air pushes against us with a force of almost fifteen pounds per square inch. When we swim under water this pressure increases. At a depth of 33 feet it doubles. And at the 100-foot level, the average skin diver is subjected to a total body pressure of nearly 150,000 pounds.

About 70 per cent of our bodies consists of liquid. These liquids are not noticeably affected by the increased pressure. However, our bodies also contain several air pockets—the lungs, the sinuses, the middle-ear cavities. Pressure does affect these hollow areas. Boyle's Law states that the volume occupied by a gas is inversely proportional to the pressure applied. Consequently the lungs of an Oriental pearl diver are compressed to half their normal size at a depth of 33 feet.

The aqualung is able to counteract this increased pressure by feeding compressed air to the skin diver at the same pressure as the water surrounding him.

The danger of air embolism occurs only when the diver rises too rapidly while holding his breath. As he rises, the water pressure against his lungs decreases and the air within his lungs expands. Unless he breathes out some of this air, his lungs will fill up like an overinflated inner tube. In rare cases known as spontaneous pneumothorax, the lungs may collapse completely.

In air embolism, however, the expanding air ruptures neighboring tissues and rushes into the blood stream. Tiny bubbles of air may enter the heart, the brain, the other vital organs. Should the bubbles become large enough to form a circulation roadblock, they may effectively stop the flow of fresh blood.

The first signs of trouble can be stiffness, dizziness, blurred speech, lack of co-ordination. Without prompt emergency treatment, the patient may then suffer unconsciousness, sudden convulsions, paralysis and—generally—death.

The only effective treatment is once again to increase pressure on the patient through recompression. The increased pressure will then compress the air bubbles, so that they will not block the flow of blood.

In this case, of course, an ounce of prevention is worth all the recompression chambers in the world. It is imperative that every beginning diver make a conscious effort to breathe out while rising toward the surface. Even experienced divers make a practice of never rising more rapidly than the bubbles flowing from their aqualungs.

A related underwater illness—the bends, or compressed-air illness—was once a prime danger for the helmeted diver. It seemed to strike divers who worked in deep water and stayed down for long periods of time. A famous French doctor, Paul Bert, discovered that this could be avoided if the diver rose more slowly to the surface.

Later research revealed that the water pressure forced nitrogen into the blood stream. This nitrogen could be released when the diver rose slowly toward the surface.

If he was hauled too rapidly, some nitrogen remained in his blood stream and formed bubbles—those dangerous roadblocks preventing the flow of life-giving blood. Today's hard-hat divers rely on decompression tables—complicated timetables that tell them how long they must remain at various levels before surfacing. No inexperienced skin diver should ever attempt a dive that demands decompression.

The most insidious of all underwater illnesses is known technically as nitrogen narcosis. Ironically, this can be both pleasant and harmless. Captain Cousteau has often called the condition "rapture of the deep."

However, this rapture can also be highly lethal. And there is no immunity; nitrogen narcosis makes no distinction between experienced diver and novice. Although its basic nature remains a medical mystery, most doctors feel that it is caused by pressurized nitrogen acting upon the central nervous system.

Many skin divers don't feel the effects of nitrogen narcosis until they reach a depth exceeding two hundred feet. However, we have experienced the mysterious "rapture" during our few brief excursions beneath the one-hundred-foot level.

The first sensations are entirely pleasurable. The spirit soars. Deadlines and similar mundane worries are forgotten. The smallest incidents become comical; the smallest tasks, difficult. The diver feels lightheaded, giddy, almost intoxicated.

At this point the diver should turn back and rise slowly toward the surface. At lower levels the sense of euphoria increases. Thoroughly intoxicated, the diver literally staggers under water. The exotic visions of a drug addict race through his mind. The basic human instinct of self-preservation vanishes; he no longer cares whether he lives or dies. In fact the very act of breathing becomes an arduous chore.

Drowning—whether through nitrogen narcosis, underwater accidents, or tragic carelessness—remains the primary killer of all skin divers. The threat of drowning can be avoided only when the skin diver learns to handle any emergency that arises.

This factor above all others points up the absolute necessity of SCUBA training. We have visited the U. S. Navy's Underwater Swimmers' School in Key West, Florida. We have attended other training programs on the French Riviera and the coast of California. We discovered that all reputable skin-diving schools place a primary and continual emphasis on safety.

Fourteen-year-old Frank Randall, completely recovered, made a belated decision to learn the proper techniques of SCUBA diving before again venturing forth on his own. We joined Frank for the classes taught by Dick Matt, the expert diver who had saved his life.

Even before attending our first class, we had to undergo an extensive physical and mental examination. Not every athlete can walk a tightrope, nor can every swimmer safely make the transition to skin diver. A permanent respiratory illness, a chronic heart condition, an illness of the middle ear—these ailments, bothersome under any conditions, can prove fatal to the skin diver. Equally dangerous can be certain mental conditions such as claustrophobia, a fear of closed-in places.

Pronounced medically fit, we were not led immediately to deep water. Our first training sessions took place in the relative safety of a high school swimming pool.

"First I want to introduce you to the tools of your trade," Dick Matt said. "Your mask must fit comfortably, offer a wide range of vision, and keep the water out. Swim fins are rigid or flexible, large or small —you'll try them all and find out which gives you the greatest power with the least amount of effort."

On our first day with Dick Matt we did not even see an aqualung. Most trainers prefer to start with the snorkel, the hollow plastic breathing tube that lets us breathe air while floating in a face-down position.

Entering the pool from the shallow side, we waded out until the water reached our waist. Breathing through the snorkel, we then practiced floating and swimming on the surface. Taking and holding deep breaths, we then attempted our first snorkel dives. In the deep end of the pool we felt a slight pain in our ears.

"That pain should not be ignored," Dick warned. "It's caused by water pressure pushing against the air trapped in your middle-ear cavities. You must learn to release this pressure by tightening your jaw muscles, chewing, swallowing saliva. Then your ears should 'pop.' "

"Would it help if we wore earplugs?" Frank Randall asked.

"Never wear earplugs," Dick Matt said. "The water pressure could force them in and puncture your eardrums. Also never dive with a cold—nasal congestion may make it impossible to clear your air passages, and this will eventually cause a serious ear infection. Ear-popping may seem difficult at first, but later on it will become a matter of second nature to you."

SCUBA divers wear weights to help them stay near ocean floor.

During our second session in the pool, we received our introduction to SCUBA (Self-Contained Underwater Breathing Apparatus). When we first saw the wide variety of aqualung sets, we felt as perplexed as kids in a candy shop. Dick Matt, familiar with the strengths and weaknesses of each brand, helped us select equipment that was both sturdy and inexpensive.

The basic aqualung consists of the following components: a tank of compressed air, tubes feeding the air into a mouthpiece, valves regulating the flow of air, a harness, and an emergency device to warn the diver when the air supply is running low.

"It's a fine invention, a splendid piece of equipment," Dick Matt told us. "But don't ever make the mistake of relying on it completely."

"What do you mean by that?" Frank asked.

"Anyone can dive with SCUBA," Dick replied. "The real trick—the reason you men are here—is to learn how to handle yourself if the SCUBA fails you. The good skin diver relies upon only one piece of equipment —himself."

Before allowing us to test our aqualungs, Dick showed us the proper techniques for measuring the supply of air in the cylinder. After checking for any possible air leaks, we then tested the demand regulator, the valvular device that supplies air to the diver.

After slipping into our fins, we then attached the aqualung harness. We learned that the straps should be snug and the metal cylinder should be placed so that there is no chance of one's head striking it during any sudden underwater movements.

There was one additional piece of equipment—lead weights attached to our belt. Our instructor explained that the weights were necessary because water tends to counteract the pull of gravity. The amount of weight used will vary from one person to another. We started off with five pounds of ballast and added more or took off some as it became necessary. A diver who does heavy work on the bottom will often find it necessary to carry a considerable amount of lead.

After coating the inside of our face masks with saliva and rinsing them in water to prevent "fogging," we fastened the masks in place. Wading slowly in from the shallow end of the pool, we tested our mouthpieces.

As we prepared to submerge for the first time, Dick called out one last, all-important reminder.

"Don't forget," he shouted. "*Never hold your breath while ascending.*"

This was our first SCUBA dive. This was the beginning.

As the summer days went by, we learned how to handle ourselves and our equipment under water. The first emphasis was on safe techniques. We learned how to enter the water from a horizontal position with a head-first surface dive. From the side of a boat we used the feet-first surface dive. We learned to master the underwater dog paddle, the breast stroke, the graceful dolphin kick and the relaxing flutter kick with our arms pinned to our sides, or held directly in front of us in murky water. We learned to conserve our air supply by breathing only once with every seven kicks.

From the pool we graduated to the calm waters of a protected inlet. As we descended to depths of fifteen and twenty, then thirty and forty feet, we learned to equilibriate the increased pressure against our ears.

And as we progressed, we were given more tools of the skin-diving trade. We learned the value of the knife —not as a weapon, but as an instrument to cut rope or seaweed that might entangle with our equipment. We were given depth gauges and compasses for orientation in deep, murky water. We learned the underwater sign language for communicating with our diving companions.

Day after day we went deeper and deeper. Our final

Buddy Breathing. Diver shares his air supply with his companion whose equipment has failed. *(U.S. Navy Photo)*

dive took us one hundred and fifty feet beneath the surface. Gaining confidence, we began to feel completely at ease in the strange new world. However, one morning near the end of our training period Dick Matt managed to shatter our confidence quite effectively with one simple statement.

"Today," he announced, "the three of you are going down with just two aqualungs."

"How will we do that?" Frank asked.

"You'll see," he replied.

This experiment was designed to show us the value of the "buddy system." Skin divers, like combat soldiers, should never undertake their mission without a companion. Should one aqualung cease working, it is a relatively simple matter for two divers to share the same air supply by taking turns using the same mouthpiece. This procedure, known as "buddy breathing," should be mastered by all divers.

In subsequent trips Dick showed us how to handle the problem of flooded breathing tubes or a flooded face mask. In each case the primary rule is to remain calm. Each problem can easily be solved by following the techniques learned by thousands of other skin divers.

Once the diver learns to protect himself, he should then learn to help others who may be in trouble. Dick showed us how to help others to shore with the arm-tow, the equipment-tow, and the hair-tow methods.

Finally, three weeks after beginning our SCUBA training, Dick took us to Manorhaven Beach. We noticed that he was not wearing his aqualung.

"You don't need me any more," he said. "You're on your own now."

"You mean we're full-fledged SCUBA divers?" Frank asked.

"That's right," he smiled. "This is your graduation day. You've learned to dive with your aqualungs and, more important, you've learned to survive if your equipment fails."

Matt offered us each a handshake and a word of congratulations. His last thought, a popular safe-driving slogan, was equally applicable to safe diving. It is a slogan that every diver, novice or veteran, should always keep in mind.

"Always be careful," he said. "The life you save may be your own."

12. Treasure Down Below

It was the stormy end of a hot July day. Directionless summer lightning flared against the yellow clouds banked above the bay. Gnats swarmed around the windswayed street lamps. The first big drops of summer rain pocked the dusty sidewalks with watery splotches.

Fourteen-year-old Frank Randall, racing against the downcoming rain, dashed up the front walk and ducked quickly beneath the shelter of the porch. We had not seen our young neighbor since completing our SCUBA training course two weeks earlier. As he greeted us, Frank released his words in short, explosive bursts of breathless excitement.

"I've got a secret," he announced. "Promise you won't tell anyone? Cross your hearts?"

We offered him our most solemn heart-crossed pledges of undying secrecy.

"Buried treasure!" he said. "Out in the bay. I just found some buried treasure!"

We were naturally skeptical. Manhasset Bay, the

home for thousands of pleasure vessels, is one of the most heavily traveled bodies of water in the world. We cautioned Frank to slow down and catch his breath.

"No kidding," he went on. "Buried treasure. It looked like a log at first. You know, sunk 'way down into the mud and all covered with barnacles. But I scraped off the barnacles and it was an old chest, the kind that the pirates used for buried gold. It was hammered together with brass nails, two rows of them."

"Did you open the chest?" we asked. "Did you look inside?"

"I couldn't do it by myself," Frank said. "That's why I came here. It's too big a job for just one man. I want you to come along with me tomorrow and give me a hand."

"Now, slow down a bit. Start from the beginning. Where did you hear about the gold? Do you mean that you just stumbled on a treasure chest?"

"Well, not exactly," he replied. "I was talking to those old-timers down at the town dock. They told me about it. They told me exactly where the chest would be."

We had often seen the "old-timers" supporting their long bamboo rods like ancient standard bearers—standing guard over the sea, standing guard over the past. At first we suspected they might be playing a prank on our youthful friend.

"But they were *right!*" Frank protested. "The chest was there, right where they said it would be. If you come with me tomorrow and help, I'll give you a share in the gold."

We quickly assured Frank that our primary interest

would be in reporting his story, not in sharing his treasure. Despite our noble intentions, however, we felt those first tingling sensations shared by all treasure hunters since the invention of money.

The summer rain, softening now, drummed gently against the shingled roof and punctuated our thoughts. Despite our natural skepticism, we were forced to admit that Frank might possibly have stumbled on something. The history of Long Island abounds in stories of sunken treasure. According to early legends, many pirates looked on this narrow strip of land as nothing more than a vast vault for their ill-gotten gains.

Captain William Kidd, the most notorious blackguard and pirate ever to hoist the skull and crossbones, is known to have cruised along the Long Island shoreline often. One of his visits gave birth to a tale that has been passed down through many generations of treasure seekers.

Similar tales, dating far back into the eighteenth century, tell of other pirates—such as the nefarious James Gillan—who buried millions of dollars worth of plunder on Long Island. Kidd and Gillan, like so many of their villainous comrades, met death on the gallows. And dead men have never been known to tell tales. The site of their entombed treasure has remained a secret, a secret perhaps forever sealed beneath the pleasant communities and luxurious estates that have since mushroomed beside the waters of Long Island Sound.

"You haven't answered my question," Frank interrupted our musings. "Will you come? Will you help me tomorrow?"

Setting his mind at ease, we assured him that he could

certainly count on our full support.

Consequently we were awakened the following morning at an unreasonable hour. Haggard and wan, Frank Randall had apparently spent a wakeful night contemplating the vast wealth awaiting him. However, he had used those sleepless hours to advantage, gathering together a wide assortment of tools: pickax, chisel, hoe, pry bar, two shovels, and several lengths of clothesline rope.

When we later saw the equipment used by experienced skin-diving treasure hunters—air lifts, power winches, jet hoses, magnetic metal detectors—we were to look back on this meager supply of garden tools with some amusement. But at the time they seemed more than adequate for our task.

Impatient, reluctant to waste valuable time on such trivial matters as breakfast, Frank grudgingly allowed us to pause for a single cup of black coffee. He then directed us to the grounds of the Manhasset Bay Yacht Club, our point of departure. After parking the car, we carried our aqualungs and treasure-hunting equipment down to the water's edge.

Two early-rising sailing enthusiasts and a seagull dozing beside the swimming pool studied our ungainly assortment of garden tools with understandable mystification.

The tide was high and the water was clear. Since our first trip was merely for reconnaissance purposes, we left the tools beyond the high-water mark and followed Frank. Sure of his directions, he submerged and rapidly assumed a northeasterly course. Within five minutes we arrived at the site of the buried treasure. The situation was precisely as Frank had described it. The chest was securely imbedded in the ooze beneath five fathoms of water. The curved upper surface of the container, covered with barnacles, protruded above the sandy bottom like a waterlogged tree trunk. We could see where Frank had scraped off some of the barnacles and uncovered a double row of tarnished brass studs.

Now thoroughly convinced that Frank Randall had not exaggerated, we hastened back for the digging tools. The actual labor of digging away the sand proved much more taxing than similar work on dry land. Before shoveling through to the chest, we exhausted two containers of compressed air.

As we dug, we noticed several disturbing facts. The exterior of the old chest seemed remarkably well preserved after several centuries beneath the sea. And, surprisingly enough, there was no trace of a lock on it. After no more than a moment's silent debate, we decided to open the chest there, instead of going through the tedious business of lugging it into shore.

Since Frank was the director of our little expedition, we granted him the privilege of prying up the cover and examining the gold. His hands slipped nervously from the metal pry bar twice as he attempted to raise the rusted lid. We watched his face closely as the cover finally gave way to his efforts.

Dismay, not jubilation, shadowed his young face as he looked into the chest. There was no pile of golden coins, no horde of long-lost jewels. There was only a plentiful supply of brackish water. And at the bottom we discovered a single sheet of stainless steel. Although

the metal was covered with green algae, we could read
the message that had been etched onto its surface.

FRIEND—
A wise man once said: "THERE IS NOTHING
SO WELL KNOWN AS THAT WE SHOULD NOT
EXPECT SOMETHING FOR NOTHING."
Kindly return this chest so that others may
learn that pleasure—not treasure—is the skin
diver's reward.
THE LONG ISLAND MUDHAWKS

As Frank read the words, his initial dismay dissolved
in a choking gale of underwater laughter. Gasping for
air, he passed the inscription along to us. Then as we
joined him in appreciation of the ingenious prank, he
carefully returned the metal plate to the bottom of the
chest. After closing it, we picked up our shovels and
took great pains to cover up all traces of our visit.

Later, exhausted, we rested on the beach and let the
midmorning sun wash over our aching muscles. Two
young SCUBA divers, friends of Frank, joined us and
asked several penetrating questions about our collection
of garden tools.

"Oh, we were just treasure hunting," Frank
explained. "We heard that there was some sunken
gold out there."

"Sunken *gold!*" The taller boy seemed interested.

"We didn't find any gold," Frank said quite truth-
fully. "It must be 'way down in the sand. It was supposed to be sixty yards north of the pier, and ten yards
due east."

"Say, Frank, would you let us borrow your shovel?"

"Sure. Help yourself."

The two young divers needed no further encouragement. With hasty farewells they picked up the shovels and waded out into the water. As they plunged beneath the surface, Frank once again collapsed with uncontrollable laughter.

"That's a fine way to treat your pals," we chided him.

"It's only fair," he protested. "After all, we don't want to be greedy. We ought to share our treasure with the rest of the world."

Our only profit from that first treasure-hunting expedition was knowledge. Many other divers learn the same lesson the same way. However, this does not stop them from trying and trying again.

The center of most SCUBA treasure hunting is in the clear, warm waters of the Caribbean and the Gulf of Mexico. Spanish explorers first sailed these waters over four centuries ago. They established colonies in the West Indies, in Mexico, and throughout South America.

The history of these early Spanish conquistadors is by no means an attractive one. It is a story of murder, plunder, and one-sided warfare. The invaders burned entire villages to the ground, enslaved the people, and carted away gold and silver that the natives had mined for centuries.

Spanish galleons, carrying an average cargo worth two million dollars, transported the treasure across the Atlantic Ocean. Over a period of three hundred years these ships carried enormous quantities of gold and silver back to Spain.

However, not all the ships in the Spanish fleet reached

their destination. Unpredictable tropical hurricanes dashed many of the slow-moving vessels against the coral reefs. One single gale swept seven ships into the Florida Keys in the year 1733. Another constant threat was the lean, hungry pirate ships that haunted the West Indies and fed on the treasure-laden galleons.

Historians estimate that two hundred million dollars' worth of Spanish gold lies off the Florida coast alone. And there are countless tons of sunken treasure scattered beneath the other seas of the world.

However, even when this treasure can be located, the actual recovery often proves difficult. Four million dollars in Philippine silver, dumped hastily during the Japanese invasion, still rests beneath the waters of Caballo Bay. A ship carrying the jewels of Marie Antoinette has been located off the Delaware shore, but swift ocean currents have hampered all salvage attempts. Similarly, divers have been unable to raise a ship carrying five million dollars in gold, although it rests beneath a mere fifty-five feet of water off the coast of Virginia.

To date less than one-tenth of the world's sunken treasure has been recovered. One of history's biggest hauls was made by an eighteenth-century Englishman, William Phipps. Using three hundred native divers and primitive wooden diving bells, Phipps managed to retrieve three million dollars' worth of Spanish gold.

The invention of the aqualung revived a widespread interest in the search for sunken treasure and gave birth to a brand-new type of adventurer, the skin-diving treasure hunter. Bermudian archaeologist Teddy Tucker has discovered the remains of two Spanish galleons within the past five years, and each find has netted him a profit of about one hundred thousand dollars. Robert Marx, a young ex-Marine, recently discovered a sunken eighteenth-century cargo ship near Yucatán, Mexico, and has thus far managed to remove fifteen thousand separate items, ranging from golden combs to ancient sewing needles.

These, however, are isolated cases. Thousands of SCUBA divers search for underwater treasure, but few ever unearth so much as a single piece of eight.

We have met many divers who were bitten by the gold bug. The most severe case we ever encountered is Walt Hammer, a successful Baltimore lawyer who flies down to Florida about a dozen times every year. During our most recent trip to Key West we boarded Walt's yacht to accompany him on one of his treasure-hunting jaunts.

"I think we're really onto something big," Walt told us. "Let's go below and I'll tell you about it."

As we followed Walt down to the cabin, his crew prepared to cast off. Once we were under way, Walt proceeded to unroll several maps of a small section of shore line on the eastern tip of the Florida peninsula.

"I think we've located the *Santa Margarita*," he said.

"The *Santa Margarita?*"

"A Spanish galleon," he said. "It sank during a storm in 1595, carrying eight million dollars' worth of silver bullion in its hold."

"What makes you think you've found the ship?"

"These" he said, pointing to the maps. "I've spoken to every historian and museum curator in Florida, trying to get the best-educated guess of where the vessel went down."

"Still, that's only a guess."

"That was only the beginning," he continued. "I then spoke to every skin diver and fisherman in the area. I asked them whether they had noticed any unusual formations on the coral reefs—anything that might be the remains of an ancient ship."

"And?"

"And no one had seen anything remotely resembling a ship. But just two days ago I met an old beachcomber who seemed to have a pretty fair idea where the ship might be."

"You mean you're going to all this trouble and expense because one old beachcomber thinks he knows where the ship *might* be?"

"Not entirely," our host said. "There was also a matter of certain evidence."

Walt Hammer answered our unasked questions by reaching mysteriously into his jacket pocket and emptying its contents onto a bunk. At first glance the small objects seemed to be discolored buttons. Closer inspection, however, revealed that they were ancient coins—silver coins that had been minted in the seventeenth century.

Walt, like young Frank Randall, had definitely been bitten by the gold bug. He had all the symptoms, all the signs of the feverish underwater malady that science has never been able to cure. And we discovered once again that it can be highly contagious.

However, this time we were not forced to rely on garden tools. Walt Hammer's sloop was equipped with a complex array of scientific equipment. The entire hunt lasted eleven days. During those eleven days we received a firsthand look at a treasure hunt that might well stand as a model for all SCUBA divers searching for sunken gold.

The most difficult part of the process was the search itself. Walt's big vessel could not be used over the treacherous reefs. And since the water often went to considerable depths, the standard glass-bottomed boat was of only limited value. Moreover, since the target area covered many square miles, it would prove impractical to search "on foot" with the aqualung.

This problem was solved with a homemade device known as a tow sled. Constructed of tubular aluminum, this underwater vehicle is towed behind a motorboat.

Tow sledding team making an underwater survey.

The pilot of the tow sled, breathing through the aqua-lung, is able to guide his highly maneuverable vehicle close to the reefs while still being able to avoid any sudden collisions.

Before even beginning the search, Walt had charted out our day-by-day schedule. Employing grid search techniques, he was towed on a straight line between two widely spaced buoys. After each trip the buoys were transplanted ten yards to the right and the entire process was repeated.

On the third day of searching, Walt found the sunken ship. Marking the spot with a quick-release buoy, Walt surfaced in the tow sled and we boated back toward the marker. Joining him beneath the water, we were vaguely disappointed by his discovery. It appeared to be nothing more significant than a mound that had been covered with coral.

This turned out to be the site of an ancient sunken ship. After several centuries of submersion the wood had been eaten by the teredo worm and rotted away. The metal fixtures—the cannons, the ballast, the cargo—had been scattered over acres of ocean bottom and effectively buried beneath a blanket of mud and seaweed and coral. The only trace of the sunken ship was the dimly recognized pattern formed by a single cannon.

The sunken ship was the object of all our attentions during the following eight days. The techniques employed by Walt almost exactly paralleled those used by the archaeologist uncovering the ancient city of Port Royal. A jet hose blasted away sand and coral. The suction device known as an air lift removed the remaining sand and washed it through a filter aboard the ship.

The filter removed the larger objects—the coins and small stones.

We would like to report that Walt Hammer actually discovered the *Santa Margarita*. However, such was not the case. At the end of our excursion we had recovered a cannon that weighed three thousand pounds, a handful of disintegrating coins, and nothing else of value. Sailing back toward Key West, we expected that Walt would be quite discouraged.

"Not at all," he informed us. "That's a splendid cannon. It should make an outstanding decoration for my lawn back in Baltimore."

"But it certainly won't repay you for all your expense and trouble during the past eleven days," we protested.

"What expense? What trouble?" he asked. "We've enjoyed eleven days of sun and sea, eleven days of exercis and skin diving. That's plenty of repayment."

He paused then and a smile was reflected in his eyes.

"Besides, I'm planning to come back here in a month or so. Maybe then I'll be able to find the right ship, the real *Santa Margarita*."

13. Scuba Scientist

THE TOOTHLESS BLACK MOUTH of an underwater cave grinned wickedly up at us through the gray lake waters. This was to be our first experience with cave diving and we hesitated uncertainly before lowering ourselves into the yawning entrance.

We were greeted by a second opening, the beginning of a horizontal-shaft tunnel. Again we hesitated before cautiously entering the narrow corridor.

Daylight was behind us now. We were swallowed up in a world of eternal night. The beams from our underwater flashlights caromed off the black ribs of rock that lined the tunnel. The only sound was the sporadic gurgle of our exhaled air bubbles. Our only companions were those characterless and sightless blobs of transparent protoplasm known as newts.

Ten minutes passed. Then fifteen. The twisting tunnel pressed more and more closely against us, enveloping us in eerie darkness.

We had taken every precaution. Still we could not

shake off the presentiment of impending danger. A laby-rinth of minor tunnels branched off from the main stem, forming a confusing maze of underground rivers. The thought of being lost in the bowels of the earth is not a comforting one; the skin diver who loses direction in a cave is living on borrowed time.

We also realized that all of our SCUBA training would be useless should our equipment suddenly mal-function. For there was no easy ascent to the surface, no chance to make repairs in the light of day.

Our watches and compasses informed us that we had arrived at our destination. We stopped then, and our skin-diving companions began to chip away with small picks samples of the rock lining the cave. The unnat-urally loud sound of the tools only emphasized the unearthly, tomblike silence.

Speleology—cave exploration—gained the status of a formal science as far back as 1913. At that time French scientists made their first descents in search of ancient fossils, rare forms of bats and insects, buried minerals. Using flexible metal ladders and tubular climbing poles, the speleologists were able to go several hundred feet beneath the light of day.

Their progress was stopped not by the end of the cave, but by the beginning of water. The first cave explorers tried to use helmet divers to break through the underground rivers, lakes, and springs. However, many of these early attempts ended tragically when sharp rocks severed air hoses, cutting off the divers from their supplies of life-giving air.

The aqualung has opened new worlds to the speleolo-gist. Carrying his air upon his back, the cave diver is

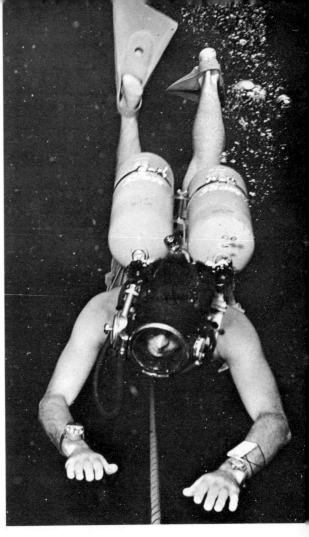

This diver-explorer wears a watch, a compass
and depth gauge on his wrists. *(Jordan Klein)*

now able to swim through the water barriers and to explore uncharted caverns and air chambers that lie beyond.

However, the peril remains great. Cave diving should never be attempted by beginners. There is no allowance for inexperience, no room for an error in judgment, no second chance.

Our first excursion into the loneliness of the subterranean world was relatively safe. We were diving beneath Connecticut's Strickland Quarry, a man-made lake that had been explored by many other divers before us. We carried flashlights, compasses, depth gauges, wrist watches, detailed charts and maps, a strictly observed timetable. A sturdy nylon rope linked us to a tender back at the surface. Moreover, our guide was an expert skin diver, a man who had made this trip many times in the past.

Despite these safety factors, we were slightly uneasy until our watches indicated that it was time to turn back. Retracing our underwater steps, we followed the guideline back to the first dim rays of reflected sunlight at the mouth of the tunnel. The quarry, flooded with sunlight, seemed unnaturally bright—a most welcome sight.

We emerged from the water with new respect for our guide, a SCUBA scientist who is equally at home within a dismal cave or a well-lighted university lecture hall. John Sanders, an associate professor of geology at Yale University, is one of many scientists who have learned to use the aqualung as a basic research tool.

As we sat on shore, Professor Sanders explained the aqualung's increasing popularity in science. His remarks were directed to the other divers, geology students at Yale who had learned how to skin-dive as part of their homework assignments. The young teacher spoke with enthusiasm and quiet eloquence.

"Geology—earth science—is concerned with pebbles and mountains, streams and oceans, specks of dust and entire deserts. In a sense, geologists are detectives. They take evidence—a grain of sand or a slab of granite—and they investigate it thoroughly. When was it born? How was it formed? What has happened to it through the centuries? What is happening to it at this moment?"

Pausing then to light his pipe, Professor Sanders glanced at the faces of his students. The fledgling scientists were silent, listening intently to his every word.

"Charles Lyell, a pioneer geologist, once complained that we would never be able to unlock the secrets of this planet because three-quarters of the world would forever be hidden beneath the ocean. But he said that back in 1830. His words were true only before the birth of the aqualung.

"Today we can complete thousands of investigations beneath the sea. We add together the results. Gradually we're beginning to solve some of the earth's basic mysteries. And gradually we're beginning to write the biography of this planet during its billions of years of existence."

Writing our planet's biography is no easy task. Scientists, the skilled investigators of our natural world, must regularly face hazards such as the danger of cave diving. Conrad Limbaugh, America's most famous marine biologist, lost his life recently while exploring a Mediterranean cave. Even the tunnel we had investigated recently claimed the lives of two young divers, teen-age boys who entered the shaft without rope, adequate lighting, or a detailed timetable.

The SCUBA scientist has perhaps enjoyed his greatest success in prospecting for underwater oil, the pools of "black gold" that lie beneath the coastal waters of California and the Gulf of Mexico. Oil, created by decomposing animal life, is often found near salt domes —mile-wide plugs of underwater salt formed during a time of great heat. And many of the larger recent oil discoveries have been found in natural subterranean hollows formed by earthquakes powerful enough to rearrange entire layers of rock.

Many skin-diving geologists have searched for oil with magnetometers and gravity meters, sensitive instruments that help them pinpoint the location of the salt domes and limestone reefs that sometimes contain oil. Others, however, use only a dandelion digger, a garden tool that enables them to gather sediment for subsequent laboratory analysis.

Thirty-five major oil companies have constructed offshore drilling platforms, the man-made islands that sometimes stand in a hundred feet of water. At this writing, nearly two hundred thousand barrels of oil are mined every day from the offshore operations.

The first SCUBA scientists were, naturally enough, men who had always investigated the sea: oceanographers, marine scientists, ichthyologists, invertebrate zoologists. Nearly all sciences—biology, chemistry, physics, botany—are now taking a closer look at the potentiality of the aqualung.

Even the seemingly unrelated fields of medicine and

space research have added the SCUBA scientist to their staffs. Underwater researchers at the Lerner Medical Laboratory in the Bahamas are delving into the cause and cure of cancer through experimentation with living fish. The Astronauts, our nation's first space pilots, accustom themselves to the weightlessness of outer space by spending many hours skin diving.

Some of the most intriguing underwater research

Underwater "eyes." Skin diver tests sonar radar to locate hidden objects. Powered by flashlight batteries the sonar set sends signals to diver's earphones on discovering object. (*U.S. Navy Photo*)

projects are those carried out by marine biologists and botanists. The world of science is openly worried about our ability to feed earth's exploding population. The problem of nourishing millions of people may someday be solved by vast underwater farms.

The oceans contain almost ten times as many plants as does the land. Most of these plants, too small to be seen with the naked eye, are harvested by the fish that we eat. The Japanese, seaweed eaters for many centuries, now regularly farm over fifty different ocean plants. And experimentation in this country has shown that a horse switched from a diet of hay to a diet of dried seaweed can gain as much as fifty pounds in less than three weeks.

One particular seaweed, known as kelp, has served man in many ways. The Scots developed kelp-burning factories many years ago, first for the manufacture of glass and then for the production of iodine. We are now able to extract a substance known as algin from kelp. Algin can be used in the manufacture of medicines, face creams, plastic wrappings, and even typewriter rollers.

Seventeen SCUBA scientists at the University of California are currently engaged in full-time research into kelp. These men are under the leadership of Dr. Wheeler North, a staff member at the Scripps Institute of Oceanography. Dr. North, an expert in the field of biological oceanography, is also a certified skin-diving instructor.

We met Dr. North aboard a research ship that had just returned from Mexico. We noticed that the ship carried a rather unusual cargo, living kelp plants.

"A very special type of kelp," Dr. North informed us. "This is one of the hardiest known types of giant kelp, a plant that flourishes along the western coasts of the United States and Mexico."

"You mean you sailed 'way down to Mexico just to harvest some kelp?"

Dr. North, a wiry, dark-haired man in his mid-thirties, smiled before answering our question.

"Not exactly," he said. "We're not harvesting this kelp; we're transplanting it. We're starting colonies of it in this area."

"What's the matter with the kelp that now grows in California waters?"

"It's dying," he said. "The temperature along these shores has been rising steadily since 1957. And much of the kelp has been unable to survive the temperature changes. This particular variety is resistant to temperature changes. It may seem like a good deal of trouble just for seaweed; however, we've discovered that many fish and sea animals like to graze in kelp areas. When the kelp disappears, the fish must seek out new underwater pastures. We are losing fish that are valuable food items. And we are also losing a plant that may someday be used for food itself."

We watched the skilled scientists as they transplanted the seaweed. This was our final dive to danger—not the danger of a man-eating shark or a sudden accident, but the danger that may face entire generations of human beings who have not yet been born.

John F. Kennedy, the President of the United States, emphasized this very danger in a speech presented during his first year in office.

"Knowledge of the oceans is more than a matter of curiosity," President Kennedy said. "Our very survival may hinge upon it."

In asking Congress to appropriate an unprecedented amount of money toward underwater research, the President then made a statement that clearly outlines the task for the SCUBA scientists of the future.

"Knowledge and understanding of the oceans promise to assume greater and greater importance in the future. This is not a one-year program—or even a ten-year program. It is the first step in a continuing effort to acquire and apply the information about a part of our world that will ultimately determine conditions of life in the rest of the world."

The story of skin diving is, after all, a story of exploration and search. It is the exploration of the three-hundred-million cubic miles of ocean and sea, river and lake. It is the search for pleasure or treasure, for health or wealth, for tranquillity or adventure.

Or it may be the noblest search of all—the search for knowledge.